D0397599

Dignity and Vulnerability

Dignity and Vulnerability

Strength and Quality of Character

George W. Harris

UNIVERSITY OF CALIFORNIA PRESS
Berkeley · *Los Angeles* · *London*

University of California Press
Berkeley and Los Angeles, California

University of California Press
London, England

Copyright © 1997 by
The Regents of the University of California

Library of Congress Cataloging-in-Publication Data
Harris, George W.
    Dignity and vulnerability : strength and quality
of character / George W. Harris.
        p.   cm.
    Includes bibliographical references and index.
    ISBN 0-520-20843-9 (cloth : alk. paper)
    1. Respect for persons—History.   2. Charac-
ter—History.   3. Dignity—History.   I. Title.
BJ1533.R42H37   1997
649'.1—dc21   96-48497
                                         CIP

Printed in the United States of America
1   2   3   4   5   6   7   8   9

The paper used in this publication is both acid-free
and totally chlorine-free (TCF). It meets the mini-
mum requirements of American Standard for Information Sciences—Permanence of Paper for Printed
Library Materials, ANSI Z39.48–1984 ♾

For Patty, my wife and friend

Contents

Preface

I began this project with a few thoughts on one topic, and they grew into many on a larger one. I wanted to say something about vulnerability and discovered that there was much to say about human dignity. Once a rather die-hard Kantian, I have made over the last decade or so a fairly radical transition to a basically Aristotelian way of thinking. Persistent thoughts over the status of personal ties in the moral life first led me away from Kant and toward Aristotle. Though I think some of the criticisms of Kant regarding friendship, for example, are misguided, in the end I do not think Kant gives us a very satisfactory way of thinking about what is most important to us in personal relationships. What Kant is supposed to give us, however, is an insightful way of thinking about human dignity and the worth of persons. I do not believe he does. In fact, I think that Kant and his predecessors, the Christians and the Stoics, deeply mislead us about our dignity. In this sense, this book is an attack on a certain tradition and what is thought to be its greatest strength. I hope, however, that what emerges is more positive than negative, that what I say provides some insight into what we actually do value in ourselves and others.

My debts are many and varied. Most I owe to my wife, Patty, and my daughters, Rachel and Jenny, for tolerating the idiosyncrasies of a husband and a father who is also a philosopher, a writer, and a sometimes distant life-form. What I owe them most is not just for their nurturing, though I certainly owe them for this, but for the subject matter of which I write, of life and what is best in it.

For critical response I owe several a deep debt of gratitude. Lawrence Blum, Keith Butler, Paul Davies, James Harris, Margaret Holmgren, Robert Kane, Noah Lemos, Andrew Melnyk—all provided written feedback on the manuscript. I am especially indebted to Paul Davies, not only for almost daily conversations but also for numerous readings of parts of the manuscript, particularly chapter 4. To Larry Becker and the members of his political philosophy discussion group, I am thankful for their discussion of chapters 1 through 3 and chapter 7. Students in two seminars I have taught here at the College of William and Mary over the last several years also helped me to formulate my thoughts. And, of course, there are the many conversations on these and similar topics that have influenced me greatly but for which I lack specific recall. For such conversations on Aristotle, Nietzsche, and friendship, I owe much, as always, to Douglas Browning, Chuck Krecz, Steven Leighton, and the late Edmund Pincoffs.

For financial support I am grateful to my home institution, the College of William and Mary, for a summer grant in 1995 and a Faculty Research Assignment for the academic year 1994–1995. I am also thankful for a Summer Research Stipend from the National Endowment for the Humanities for the summer of 1994.

CHAPTER I

Strength and Quality of Character

Out of life's school of war: What does not destroy me, makes me stronger.
　　　　　　　—*Friedrich Nietzsche,* Twilight of the Idols

The peculiar beauty of human excellence just is its vulnerability.
　　—*Martha Nussbaum,* The Fragility of Goodness

Moralists of various sorts use the terms "human dignity" and "human worth" often, but frequently these words have little more than rhetorical effect, even among professional philosophers. The fact is that we have a fairly vague concept of human worth and dignity, though there is a core that is instructive. What we value so much about ourselves is a question open to only somewhat vague answers, and admitting this is the first step in greater human understanding. Yet on the tradition I will criticize, the idea of human worth and dignity is perfectly clear. If I am right, this is a mistake. We need not only to rethink what our deepest values are in regard to ourselves, we need also to recognize that when rhetoric conceals the lack of understanding or creates the illusion of its presence *philosophical* inspiration is lost.

　　There is a view of the dignity and worth of persons that goes back through Kant and Christianity to the Stoics. According to this tradition, when character either weakens or succumbs to life's troubles, it fails because it lacks the kind of strength ideal character should have. To be sure, good people are almost always less than ideal. For this reason, we understand that certain failures of strength are compatible with being a good person. Still, we would be better were we to realize fully that which gives us our dignity, and if we did fully realize our dignity we would have unlimited strength to cope with life's troubles whatever they might be. Were we good Kantians and more rational, were we good Christians and more faithful to God, and were we good Stoics and less attached to things external to our character, we would not be vulnerable to failures of strength. Being more dignified, we would be stronger.

The purpose of *Dignity and Vulnerability* is to challenge this view and to argue that on reflection we do not believe it. I will argue that this tradition does not capture our actual values regarding character and human dignity; indeed, it cuts deeply across them. Sometimes character breaks down, not because of some shortcoming in it, but because of what is good about it, because of its quality, because of the features of character that give us our dignity. Being more dignified, then, does not always make us stronger. Our most deeply held judgments about the worth of persons—vague as that concept is—are best accounted for on values indicative of pre-Hellenistic thinkers, particularly Aristotle, rather than on those views within the Stoic-Christian-Kantian tradition. In terms of what we actually value in ourselves and others, I will argue, we are far more Greek than Christian, despite the long tradition of Christianity and its more recent Kantian progeny. Moreover, our deepest values reflect the fact that we value ourselves as natural organisms, as animals, rather than as gods that transcend nature.

I.

According to the Stoic-Christian-Kantian tradition, virtues are admirable character traits that enable us to control our contrary inclinations to living a good life or to doing our duty. On this view, any failure of character is a failure of strength. Nietzsche, who was in most ways unrepresentative of the tradition, once suggested that difficult events do not destroy those with the best character but only serve to make the admirable even stronger. The emphasis is on understanding the virtues in terms of their strength: inadequate virtue is inadequate strength of character, and inadequate strength of character is inadequate virtue.

Few who have this view, however, would argue that strength is the only good-making feature of character.[1] Indeed, it is questionable that such a view is even coherent. That courage is the strength of character to control one's fear in the face of danger is both clear and coherent enough; but that loyalty in friendship is merely the strength of character to avoid the temptation to betrayal is puzzling at best. For loyalty includes not only a certain strength but also a quality of caring about one's friend. Moreover, the strength involved in loyalty and similar traits finds its virtue in the intrinsic value of this quality of caring. The more general evidence for this is the fact that the strength of character to pursue malevolent ends in the face of contrary benevolent inclination is not a virtue.

Still one might admit that quality and strength of character are distinct features and nonetheless maintain that virtues are traits that enable us to control our contrary inclinations to doing the right thing or to living a good life. On such a view, it is still true that inadequate virtue involves inadequate strength of character: given any good-making quality of character, virtue increases with the strength of the capacity for controlling contrary inclination to acting on that quality. Thus any failure of character is either the lack of a good-making quality or the inadequate strength to act on that quality. Kant's view takes this form. Doing one's duty is not enough; it must be done from the proper motive. Yet any failure to do one's duty is either not one's fault at all or is a lack of strength of one's will. The good will, then, provides at once both the appropriate quality of character and adequate strength to resist whatever contrary inclination stands in the way.[2]

How could a view that sounds so plausible be wrong? I will argue that this conceptual model for understanding the virtues is mistaken because it puts too much emphasis on strength of character and too little on its quality. Specifically, I will pursue the possibility that fragility of character is essential to many of the qualities of character we value most. If I can establish this, then it will not be true that inadequate strength of character is always inadequate virtue.

That human character is sometimes fragile in ways that we lament is undeniable. "If only he or she had more courage," we sometimes say, implying the criticism that courage is lacking where it should be found. On other occasions, the same comment might not imply a criticism at all. Rather it might reflect the thought that, despite the understandable inability to control the fear of a truly horrifying danger, more courage would be exceptionally admirable. Prisoners of war facing threats of unbearable torture come to mind. These are two ways, then, in which a character can be fragile: one involves a vice, and the other, the absence of a truly exceptional quality. Yet in neither case is fragility a good thing; for in both cases it is a weakness that could be eliminated without damage to a person's character.

Therefore, if there is another kind of fragility that is good and admirable, it is not a vice and it cannot be eliminated without damage to a person's character. I can confirm that there is this third kind of fragility, I believe, by establishing two points. The first is that there are admirable character traits that can be the source of a person's self-destruction. The

second is that the prevention of such self-destruction by the removal of
the character trait would be a greater damage to a person's character
than the self-destruction. This is because in some contexts self-destruction is the manifestation of what is good in a person's character. An alternative strategy, to which I will also appeal, is to argue that there are
admirable character traits that can be the source of making persons less
strong than they could be and that the prevention of this kind of weakness by the removal of such traits would be a greater damage to their
character than the vulnerability itself.

The kind of self-destruction and vulnerability I have in mind involves
a breakdown in a person's integrity. This might occur in several ways:
a loss in the will to live, deep clinical depression, insanity, hysteria,
debilitating shame, pervasive self-deception. The idea is not that integral breakdown is simply a form of severe discomfort. Rather it is a
form of personality disintegration that renders the person dysfunctional as an agent. This is why integral breakdown must be understood
in clinical psychological terms rather than hedonically. For instance,
nothing about the concept of pain, however intense, itself implies a
dysfunctional state of the agent, but the concept of integral breakdown
does. Duration might vary from temporary to permanent, but such
breakdown is always severe. Fragility, therefore, is the disposition of
character to experience such integral breakdown under conditions of
stress.[3]

In some stressful contexts, a person breaks down because he or she
possesses admirable character, not for the lack of it. This is especially
so regarding the virtues associated with various modes of caring, where
the expression of care is prevented. That one cares but can do nothing to help or can only do something that results in harm is the source
of tremendous stress. An understanding of the dispositions to break
down under various stressful circumstances provides insights into
the nature of admirable character traits. Moreover, these insights into
virtue cannot be revealed from the perspective of strength of character alone. I want to investigate how this applies to the character of a
person who cares in a variety of ways. Of special concern is the personally loving individual who is also respectful and sympathetic regarding others and who has the virtues of fairness, benevolence, and loyalty. What are the forms of fragility, as dispositions to integral breakdown, that are part of the character of this kind of person? This is my
central question.

II.

When we admire things, we admire them for what we take them to be, and sometimes we do not admire things for what we take them not to be. Some people, for example, admire diamonds but do not admire rhinestones. These people—at least those I have in mind—do not admire rhinestones because rhinestones look like diamonds (at least from afar) but are not. Looking like a diamond is not enough; it must be a diamond. Yet what is it for a stone to be a diamond rather than just to look like a diamond? The answer is to be found, in part, in the dispositional properties of the stone.[4] If a stone does not have certain dispositional properties, it is not a diamond. This is part of our conception of which stones are rhinestones and which are diamonds. The dispositional properties of diamonds are such that a diamond has a certain measure of hardness on a Rockwell Scale in excess of that of a rhinestone. Diamonds, for example, are hard and strong enough to cut rhinestones, but rhinestones are not hard and strong enough to cut diamonds. In this sense, the hardness of a stone is a function of its strength. People who value diamonds rather than just things that look like them apparently value this fact about their strength. For them, if stones could be synthetically produced that were visually indistinguishable from the highest-quality diamonds but did not have this measure of hardness and strength, then they would not be diamonds and valuable as such.

Other people admire good wine in ways similar to the admiration afforded to diamonds by diamond lovers. That is, they admire wine for what they take it to be rather than simply for how it appears to them through a limited set of the senses. For diamond lovers, a stone must have more than certain visual qualities: looking like a diamond is not enough. For wine lovers—at least those I have in mind—a liquid must not only taste like wine, it must be wine. If a liquid tasting like the finest Bordeaux were found in a natural spring, it could not knowingly be the object of the wine lover's admiration. Why? Because it is not wine. Part of the reason it is not wine is because it is not the product of a wine maker. Wine is an artistic product and is appreciated as such by those who admire it. Again, this is true of the admirers of wine that I have in mind. Therefore, not just anything that tastes like wine is wine.

Another reason the winelike spring water is not wine is because it is not composed of the appropriate materials. Jesus may have turned water into something that tasted like wine, but he did not turn it into wine unless he slipped in the proper ingredients. Suppose scientists could synthetically produce a liquid with the appearance and taste of an excellent Chateau Margaux but without the vulnerability to decomposition that wine has. We would perhaps come to admire and enjoy the product of their labor, but it would not be the same as the wine lover's admiration of good wine. Wine—good or bad—is both a product of a wine maker and a product composed of materials with certain dispositional properties. It is not just that wine tastes best when stored and served at certain temperatures. It is also that the taste associated with wine is made possible by the achievements of the wine maker as an artist working with materials that are subject to limitations. These limitations are internal to the dispositional properties of the materials as displayed under conditions involving temperature and other variables. If a liquid is not subject to turning into vinegar under certain environmental conditions, it is not wine. Moreover, it is a part of what wine lovers value in wine that it is vulnerable to such decomposition under these conditions. Otherwise, wine lovers would have the same appreciation for the scientist's synthetic product that they have for wine.

Among the virtues of a stone from the perspective of diamond lovers is its strength. If a stone has dispositional properties such that its character would break down under certain conditions, it is not a diamond and cannot be admired as such. By contrast, among the virtues of wine from the perspective of wine lovers is its fragility. If a liquid has dispositional properties such that its character would not break down under certain conditions, it is not wine and cannot be admired as such. The admiration of human character is both like the admiration of diamonds and like the admiration of good wine. This is to say that we admire human character both for its strength and for its fragility.

There is, however, an important sense in which the value of good character is even more connected to fragility than good wine. At some point in the life of a good wine it is still good but not as good as it was. Thus when a wine begins to break down but is not yet vinegar but wine, even good wine, its value decreases. With good character, perhaps unique in this regard, this need not be true.[5] The loving parent weakened by grief over the tragic death of her child is not less good in her state of disability. The very qualities that made her a good mother and a good person in happier times are the ones, as we shall see, that take their toll in times of misfortune.

III.

Both the strength and the fragility of an entity are features of its integrity, at least when the entity can be thought of meriologically. Only those things we think of as wholes can we think of as having integrity, for integrity involves the integration of parts in a stable whole. The strength of a diamond is one constitutive element of its integrity. A stone is not a diamond unless it has the strength to resist fracture under a certain degree of stress. Diamonds, however, also have a point at which they lose the capacity to retain the status as the wholes they are. Besides a limitation threshold on their capacity to resist the stress that measures the strength associated with hardness, they have a melting point. This is a limitation threshold that measures their incapacity to resist the stress of temperature. A diamond, then, is strong relative to the kinds of stress it has the capacity to resist under certain environmental conditions. It is fragile relative to the kinds of stress it cannot resist and remain a diamond.

The limitation threshold that measures fragility—for diamonds or anything else—is the point of integral breakdown. The qualities a thing has in virtue of which we are willing to attribute integrity to it are its categorical qualities. By reaching the limits of its capacities to retain its categorical qualities under stress, integral breakdown occurs along the lines of the limitation threshold, and integrity is lost. Integral stress is the stress put on a thing that threatens its capacity to retain its categorical qualities, and integral strength is the overall capacity of a thing to resist integral stress. I will argue that whatever a perfectly admirable human character would involve, it would not include unlimited integral strength. If this is true, then some categorical qualities of a perfectly admirable human character are admirable for their fragility.

IV.

For some virtues, there is no point of integral breakdown internal to the concept of the virtue itself. Courage, for example, does not have internal to it a necessary point of integral breakdown. This is not to deny that a person loses the status of being courageous if he or she yields to the stress of fear under certain conditions. To be fragile in this way is to lack courage. To say that there is no point of integral breakdown for a particular character trait is to assert something about meaningfully ascribing that character trait to a person. It is that nothing about thoughts of a person's having that character trait requires thoughts of integral breakdown under some conceivable conditions of stress. The point, then, is not about the necessity of ascribing fragility to those who lack courage but about the necessity of ascribing fragility to those who possess it. Lacking courage and having the vice of cowardice can be ascribed to a person only if a disposition to some degree of breakdown under certain stressful conditions can be ascribed to that person. On the other hand, having courage can be ascribed to a person without ascribing any disposition to breakdown under any conceivable stressful conditions. A person is courageous in terms of strength of character alone. There is nothing about fragility that is central to the categorical qualities of the courageous person. Of course, not all control of fear in the face of danger is courage. As Aristotle said, some such control of fear is simply foolhardiness, but when the courageous person does not control fear in foolhardy contexts, his or her fragility in such contexts is not a measure of courage. Being overcome by fear in some dangerous situations is not a sign of cowardice. Nor is not being overcome by fear in some dangerous situations a sign of courage. It is possible, however, that a person can be both courageous and foolhardy. A person, for example, might have the capacity to control fear in the face of danger in both foolhardy and nonfoolhardy contexts, as well as engage in both courageous and foolhardy behavior. The courageous person, then, can be indefinitely strong, although he or she need not be. That is, the kinds of integral stress to which courage is the response is something the perfectly courageous person is completely capable of resisting.

Moreover, the presence of courage never causes integral breakdown. If the control of fear causes integral breakdown, it is foolhardiness rather than courage. For this reason, any breakdown due to lack of courage is open to regret in the sense that these breakdowns are always preventable with more courage. Call virtues that are in principle of unlimited strength in this sense heroic virtues. One can never have "too much" of such virtues, because they deal with stress but do not generate it; and where the incapacity to deal with stress is traceable to the lack of such virtues, "more" of such virtues always aids in dealing with the stress.

Relative to heroic virtues, then, there are two kinds of integral breakdown. The first is where a character breaks down under integral stress that the minimally admirable agent is thought capable of resisting. This is the coward who is vulnerable to the stress of fear in a way that precludes having integrity in the due course of ordinary life with its normal threshold of danger. The thought here is that in the normal course of life agents face certain kinds of challenges they must successfully meet if they are to have and retain their integrity. Some of these challenges require virtues of the heroic sort with the degree of integral strength for success in ordinary circumstances. To have the capacity to control fear in the face of danger to this degree, for example, is to have the heroic virtue of courage. To lack this capacity is to have the vice of cowardice. Since the extent to which a person possesses vices measures a lack of integrity, call an integral breakdown due to vice a malignant breakdown.

To have a heroic virtue, however, is not necessarily to have it at full strength. One has a heroic virtue if one has it to a degree sufficient for integrity in the normal course of life's everyday stress. To have such a virtue at full strength is to have it to a degree to resist any stress, however extreme. To lack a virtue at full strength but to possess it at sufficient strength for normal stress is not to possess a vice. This is why a person can have courage but nonetheless lack it to some degree without being a coward. An integral breakdown due to extreme stress to a heroic virtue is not a malignant breakdown, since it is not due to vice. Call it a nonvicious breakdown.

The view under critical assessment here says that human character is always a matter of strength. It says that all failures of character are either malignant or nonvicious.

V.

In contrast with heroic virtues are virtues of care. These virtues do have a point of integral breakdown internal to them; they cannot be conceived as indefinitely strong; and they can be the source of self-destruction for an agent. Unlike heroic virtues, they do not always deal with stress but sometimes generate it. Moreover, when stress is traceable to such a virtue, "more" of the virtue often only increases the stress. Yet these virtues are among those in terms of which we find persons most admirable. If I am right about this, then virtue is the source of integral breakdown under some kinds of stress, and we can call such a breakdown a benign breakdown. It is benign because it issues from the presence of something good in the agent.

Virtues, in general, I will speak of as the capacities of agency relevant to a person's making commitments and maintaining them under stress. Since a person's deepest commitments are definitive of his or her character and integrity, we may call them categorical commitments. Virtues, then, that enable a person to maintain categorical commitments under stress are integrity-enabling capacities. The virtues of care are the integrity-enabling capacities of persons with categorical commitments founded on their caring about others, themselves, and their activities. In these terms, my thesis is that virtues of care are not of unlimited integral strength.

Since there are different modes of caring, there are different virtues that enable an agent to maintain the various kinds of commitment involved in the diversity of caring. Respecting people worthy of respect is one mode of caring, and fairness is an integrity-enabling capacity of those whose respectfulness is among their categorical qualities. Sympathizing with the plight of others is also a mode of caring, and the virtue of benevolence serves the sympathetic person just as fairness serves the respectful one. The personally loving individual needs the capacity of loyalty. Without it, the special commitments of personal love are meaningless. Caring, then, is diverse, and so are the virtues that serve it.

The diversity of the virtues of care is complicated not only by the fact that there is a diversity of ways of caring. It is also complicated by the fact that any particular mode of caring can be subject to a diversity of kinds of stress. Both loyalty and patience, for example, are expressions of the caring of personal love, but they are responsive to different kinds of stress. Patience responds to the stress of frustration, and loyalty to the stress of competing interests that threaten to undermine personal trust. It should not be surprising to find this diversity true of other modes of caring as well. In what follows, I will try to illustrate my thesis regarding strength and quality of character in a way that is sensitive to both the diversity of modes of caring and the kinds of stress to which caring is vulnerable. I will also show how my thesis bears on the question of human dignity.

VI.

The remainder of the book can be divided into three groups of chapters: chapters 2 and 3, chapters 4 through 6, and chapters 7 through 9. The first group addresses issues involved in loyalty and personal love. Chapter 2 presents a case for a special form of benign breakdown—as a response to one's former bad character. Chapter 3 deals with another kind of breakdown involving personal love where the events leading to breakdown do not involve the agent's having acted wrongfully. The second group of chapters deal exclusively with Kant and the concept of human dignity associated with his thought. Attention will be given not only to Kant himself but to contemporary Kantians as well.[6] The main target of my assault will be the concept of pure practical reason as the locus for our intrinsic worth. I will argue that a good will is best understood not as a function of the capacity for pure practical reason but, to a significant degree, of pathological features of our agency. The final chapters go back to the Stoics and Epicureans. The focus will be on recent treatment of these thinkers as a source for our own self-understanding.[7] I will argue, especially against Martha Nussbaum, that post-Aristotelian, Hellenistic thought about the worth of persons is not the source of insight she believes it to be. Indeed, these schools begin the mistake about our worth that culminates in Kant. Specifically, I will argue that this tradition misses central features of our concept of human worth by seeking a therapy that completely eliminates the vulnerability to integral breakdown. Finally, the last chapter suggests an alternative account of strength of character and of how good people can also be strong.

CHAPTER 2

Personal Love, Loyalty, and Malignant Breakdown

Loyalty in personal love is an integrity-enabling capacity responsive to a limited range of stress factors bearing on the trust relation between lover and beloved. Sometimes this involves only the interests of the lover and the beloved, but at other times it involves the interests of third parties. When it does involve third parties, the agent might care about the third party in a number of ways, which might include personal love, respect, and sympathy, or the agent might be indifferent, even hostile to the third party. The thought here is that when an agent fails in loyalty, as opposed to some other failing, the agent has betrayed the trust of a loved one to someone else's interests. This can involve one's greed, jealousy, ambition, other loyalties, sympathies, and sense of fairness. I will argue in this and the following chapter that personal loyalty is a virtue of care rendering the agent vulnerable to benign integral breakdown. Specifically, in this chapter, I will argue that it is at least plausible that some breakdowns are responses to former bad character involving personal love and that they are benign.

The argument has the structure of an argument by elimination in the following sense. Clear cases of integral breakdown will be isolated. How, then, is any particular case to be understood? Is it a malignant breakdown, a severe psychological dysfunction due to a vice? Is it a nonvicious breakdown, a dysfunction due to the lack of an exceptional virtue? Or is it benign, a dysfunction that is due to what is good about the agent and that cannot be remedied either by eliminating a vice or by adding an exceptional virtue? As cases are considered, the task is to determine if there is any plausible analysis on which the breakdown could have been prevented by the prior removal of a vice or by the presence of an exceptional virtue. To the extent to which a case resists analysis as either malignant or nonvicious and assuming that the stress is to something we admire, we are justified in concluding that the breakdown is benign.[1]

I.

Any reasonable person would admit, I believe, that love can be the source of integral breakdown, that is, that there are persons who have suffered integral breakdown where the breakdown would not have occurred had the person not been attached to others in deeply loving ways. One does not have to be a sentimentalist to admit this. Still, simply pointing to this fact does not establish my thesis. What one needs are clear cases of integral breakdown that are benign rather than malignant or nonvicious.

Consider a case of malignant breakdown. What I have in mind here is not a case in which the loving is a bad thing, though whether there are such cases is in itself an interesting topic that I will not pursue. Rather what I have in mind is a case in which the breakdown could have been prevented by the absence of either of two antecedent factors: the love or a relevant vice. What I imagine in this case is that the love is really love, not some sentimental simulacrum, and that the love is a good thing. Without the love as it is, there would be no integral stress. This is why removing it prior to the stress would prevent the threat of breakdown. There is something, then, about the love along with other elements in the situation that puts the agent under stress, and this something about the love is admirable. Yet the breakdown is malignant rather than nonvicious or benign.

One possibility to consider is that the agent is not loving enough. Indeed, it might be that the agent's love is lacking in strength. Some degree of strength, after all, is included in our conception of what it is to be a loving person. If because of weakness someone is simply never able to stand up to any degree of stress, however slight, for the sake of another, then that person simply is not a loving person. At most, such feeble emotion is mere sentimentality, but what I am trying to imagine is love rather than sentimentality, yet it is not love enough.

The difficulty is in imagining how the love could be strong enough to generate the stress but too weak to withstand it without imagining the status of some other relevant variable. Of course, it is possible to imagine that the love is strong enough to generate the stress but the presence or absence of some other factor hinders the agent from acting on that love. Consider addictions, for example. An alcoholic is caught between his addiction and the trust of his family. If his commitment to his family is categorical, as we would expect in a loving person, then when his addiction comes into conflict with the basic welfare of his family, he will, if deeply addicted, experience integral stress. It is a serious misunderstanding of some alcoholics, though it might not be of others, to think that they simply lack sufficient love for their families to overcome their addictions. Those who lack such love are those who do not experience integral stress of this sort. Yet the stress for an alcoholic of the sort I have in mind yields the tortuous thought that he cannot be trusted by his loved ones with their most important interests.

What we should say of this kind of case is that there is enough love, but also present is the addiction as a competing factor. What is absent, however, is the desirable quality of self-control or temperance, with intemperance[2] filling the void. Integral breakdowns due to conflicts of this sort, therefore, are malignant, not because of a lack of love, but because of the presence of another vice. Still, the prior removal either of the love or the vice would have prevented the breakdown. Yet surely few would advocate promoting the psychological well-being of alcoholics through a method that removes their loving dispositions. This would be at once both to harm them and to make them worse persons.

But how is this kind of case tied to the concept of loyalty? It seems rather tied to the concept of temperance. What invites this objection, I believe, is the predilection to thinking of virtue terms as names for simple abilities. If we think of loyalty, loosely, as the integrity-enabling capacity to maintain commitments of trust to loved ones, we need not think of loyalty as some simple ability.[3] Rather the capacity for maintaining categorical commitments to loved ones against competing interests is a complex capacity involving multiple abilities. Indeed, we might even say that the virtue of loyalty is a complex virtue involving a cluster of virtues as they bear on particular commitments. In this way, some cases of intemperance are also cases of disloyalty. Think of the addicted gambler who spends his child's college funds to pay off a loan in order to continue the betting habit. This is at once both intemperance and disloyalty. If we add to the example the element of fear regarding the consequences of not repaying the loan, disloyalty takes the form of cowardice. Of course, not all cases of intemperance and cowardice are cases of disloyalty. Nevertheless, to possess the virtue of loyalty one must possess a cluster of virtues that enables one to maintain one's loving and trusting commitments. Otherwise, one is subject to malignant breakdown.

There are two important points to note from this. The first is that breakdowns of this sort are failures of strength and thus do not confirm my thesis. The second is about temperance and courage as examples of what I have called heroic virtues. Note that in this context these heroic virtues are in the service of a virtue of care, namely, that of personal love. Yet in other contexts courage, temperance, and like virtues might serve other kinds of commitments, some of which might involve modes of caring and some of which might not. In this sense, heroic virtues are multifunctional virtues, but loyalty as I am construing it here is not a multifunctional virtue: it only serves the agent's care and commitment to his or her loved ones. This is why a failure in courage might not be a failure in loyalty. Indeed, it might not be a failure in caring at all.

II.

Now consider the possibility of nonvicious breakdown. These are cases where integral breakdown occurs due to the lack of exceptional virtue but without the presence of vice. That there are such cases should need little or no argument. Yet there are conceptions of morality that leave no place for such phenomena. Some consequentialist conceptions of morality, for example, leave no place for supererogation,[4] actions that go beyond the call of duty. On these views, any failure to attempt to bring about the best available state of affairs due to agent breakdown is malignant: one ought to have had better and stronger character. Julia Annas has pointed out that there appears to be an analogous problem for eudaimonistic conceptions of morality.[5] How can a breakdown due to integral stress regarding someone's attempt at living the best life available be anything other than malignant? I will not attempt to resolve this issue here. Rather I will simply assume that there is a rationale for a conception of morality that makes a place for the thought that the lack of exceptional virtue is not a vice. As I write, it is Memorial Day, and it seems to reduce a moral theory to silliness to suggest that there was not something exceptionally admirable about those brave men who struggled ashore on Omaha Beach in 1944 to stop the Nazis. Indeed, our gratitude reflects this. Thus it seems anything but philosophical insight to suggest that those of us who might not have been able to face such danger are simply cowards.

Imagine then a case where it is plausible to say that a person undergoes integral breakdown of the relevant sort. This requires that the agent is an admirable agent, without a relevant vice, yet vulnerable to integral stress because of a lack of an exceptional virtue. For example, think of the psychological makeup of a young American male in the mid-1940s who very much loved his country and fellow citizens, who was both sympathetic with and respectful of the victims of Nazi oppression yet lacked the capacity for exceptional physical courage. Add to this that he believed in the war effort, that he underwent military training designed to reinforce his resolve, and that he subsequently found himself thrust ashore at Normandy. Faced with actual combat of the most horrifying sort, however, he utterly breaks down psychologically in the midst of battle, directly causing avoidable casualties. How are we to imagine his response to this episode in his life if he is as we have described him? Here I am not thinking of his response on the field of battle but his subsequent reaction to that response and its consequences. That is, I am thinking about the response involving the thought that he had betrayed a trust for his own safety; he let his country down, leaving others in the lurch.

The range of responses is limited, and this is an important fact about empirical psychological concepts. Without some notion of integral threshold we are unable to ascribe these qualities. Here the point is not simply the empirical fact that when care is bottled up with no avenue of expression or when its only means of expression causes harm it exerts stress on the caring individual, though this is true. Rather it is a truth about psychological concepts that they attribute dispositional properties to an agent and thus an integral threshold. What that threshold is may be vaguely implied, but it is implied nonetheless.

If we imagine that the soldier lightly dismisses the response on the battlefield without any lasting effects, we can only wonder about his commitments. Of course, self-deception might prevent his seeing the magnitude of what he has done; but this would imply either that he was not loving, respectful, or sympathetic enough or that the stress of his caring in these ways together with some weakness of character has led to self-deception as a relief from the stress. But if this is the response, there seem to be good reasons for saying that self-deception of this sort is itself a malignant breakdown. It is a breakdown because it fractures the whole of character at the core, and it seems malignant because of its fundamental duplicity.

One might object, however, that integral breakdown due to self-deception is not always malignant. Being self-deceived in this case or in

similar cases might have the effect of relieving the agent of needless suffering without bringing with it some vice. Here the thought might be that
the capacity for truthfulness with oneself is heroic in the same sense in
which courage is. Just as not having courage at full strength is not a vice,
neither is having the capacity for truthfulness with oneself at full strength
a vice. Some degree of self-deception is, then, on this view consistent with
not having a vice.

The problem with this response is that a person who does not have
courage at full strength but has it at adequate strength is still courageous.
There is no analogue to this in this kind of case of self-deception, though
there might be in others. To be sure, we can have the virtue of truthfulness with ourselves and not have it at full strength, but not having it at
full strength cannot have the result of a fundamentally flawed view of
who we are at our core. Lacking the ability to see ourselves for what we
are at the core can hardly be consistent with possessing the virtue of
truthfulness with ourselves. This is why this kind of truthfulness is such
a demanding virtue. So if we imagine that the limitation threshold is
reached at the point of self-deception, we are left thinking of the response
as a malignant breakdown.[6]

Thus if we are to think of the soldier as loving, respectful, and sympathetic enough, as not responding with self-deception, and as not possessing a relevant vice, can we think of him as avoiding integral breakdown as a response to the episode on the battlefield? I cannot see how
we can. To be sure we need not imagine the breakdown as permanent,
but it must be severe and somewhat protracted, or we simply are not
imagining the kind of person with whom we started our example.

Still this does not confirm my thesis. For it is a case of nonvicious
rather than benign breakdown. Nevertheless, it represents an important
step in seeing how cases of benign breakdown are possible. In cases of
malignant breakdown, we saw that caring can bring stress to bear on
character, and if there are vices where there should be virtues integral
breakdown will occur. On the other hand, we have seen that there are
contexts in which nonvicious breakdown will occur as a result of the
stress of caring, even if there is no relevant vice but only the lack of an
exceptional virtue. In the particular case we imagined, there was the initial nonvicious breakdown on the battlefield and the subsequent breakdown as a response to the previous breakdown. The reason that an
understanding of nonvicious breakdown represents an important step in
understanding benign breakdown is this: we not only sympathize with
the soldier's subsequent response; we admire this kind of vulnerability

to a failing. For without this kind of response, we are left wondering what the relevant vice is. Did he simply not care all along? Was he too vulnerable to self-deception?

III.

From this perspective, we can look back to malignant breakdowns and forward to those that are benign. Looking back to malignant breakdowns, we can see a kind of vulnerability we admire in some cases similar to the case of the soldier, although they might involve forms of caring other than personal love.[7] Think of Oscar Schindler as represented in the film *Schindler's List*. By no means was Schindler without moral flaws. He was a philanderer, overly concerned about wealth, and at the start of the war largely indifferent to the effects of the war on its victims, especially the Jews. Exposure, however, gradually evoked sympathy and then respect for his Jewish workers and resolve and cunning against the Nazis. At the end of the war he was responsible for saving hundreds of Jewish lives. The film represents his character in a revealing scene as the workers are being freed from their forced labor and suffering. In the face of their gratitude for his efforts, he sees that there was more that he could have done had he been less vain. Had he not maintained the use of an expensive automobile, an elaborate wardrobe, even costly fountain pens, he could have financed the salvation of a few more lives. As these thoughts about his extravagance and vanity pour in on him, he is overcome not only by his sense of shame but also by his sense of caring.

To my knowledge Schindler never experienced integral breakdown, but he did experience integral stress in this particular scene. This is a fact that we admire about him. That is, we admire the fact that he was vulnerable to stress as a response to viewing the weaknesses of his character, especially where thoughts about those weaknesses are combined with care and regret. Had he experienced breakdown, however, it would have been due to vices in the sense that the stress would have been avoidable had he not been so vain. Do we call this a malignant or a benign breakdown?

For a breakdown to be benign, it must be a case where the caring is the internal source of the stress, where there is no relevant vice, and where we cannot imagine an exceptional virtue that would allow the agent to deal with the stress in a way that avoids the breakdown. If these conditions hold, then the only way to avoid the breakdown would be to remove the caring, which would be to eliminate something central to the value of the agent's character. How does this apply to Schindler, if we imagine him to have broken down?

To be sure, so imagined he could have avoided the integral stress when looking back had the truth of his character been different, that is, had he not been so vain. Yet what we are evaluating is the state of his character at the point of reflection. Imagine that he is not at this point any longer vain. He is not regretting that he is vain but that he was vain. How do we remove the stress? It is not by removing the vanity, for it is no longer there; it is not by removing the thought that he was vain, for that would be allowing self-deception; and it is not by removing the caring, for that is a source of what is good about him. The only thought left within the model of malignant breakdown is to locate another relevant vice. But what is it?

We might think of him as a coward, but this thought no sooner occurs than it evaporates. How is he a coward if his thoughts about what he has been and its costs to others crush him? It would seem that for cowardice to get a foothold here, we would need to introduce self-deception generated by the fear of self-appraisal; but there is self-appraisal of the sort inconsistent with self-deception. Indeed, the presence of self-knowledge here seems to testify to courage in this regard.

Another possibility is the kind of self-indulgence found in self-pity. Three responses come quickly to mind here. The first is that self-pity might lead to psychological breakdown of the sort in question, but it is not itself necessarily a form of such breakdown. Second, self-pity is not a response generated by caring of the sort we imagine Schindler to have at this point. Finally, we do not have to imagine self-pity to imagine the breakdown.

Another possibility is something we might call despairingness or unhopefulness about the future, where these are names for the vice of yielding too readily to pessimism. Faced with the future, he firmly believes that his former vices will return, causing harm to others, and he cannot live with that responsibility. So construed, this is closely akin to a case of cowardice. Yet it is not so much that he cannot face his fears than that he firmly believes that there is no hope for his character and its consequences.

Now it does seem that if his unhopefulness or despair is generated by fear of responsibility, self-pity, or something other than a rational assessment of the facts about himself, then this would be a case of malignant breakdown, for it would be due to self-deception. If, however, the despair is due to a rational assessment of the facts, it seems that this also makes it a rather odd but illuminating case of malignant breakdown. On this alternative, the breakdown is malignant because it is avoidable with stronger character: one does not have to despair about one's vanity if one is not vain. It is interesting, though, because the breakdown is an expression of what is good about him. Were he not caring, he would be indifferent to such a flaw, and this is an important fact about some forms of malignant breakdown: even they sometimes reveal what is good about an agent. Yet, despite the fact that on this analysis the breakdown is malignant (even if interesting), the point remains that we can imagine the breakdown without imagining cowardice, self-indulgence, or unhopefulness. Showing that it could be malignant is not showing that it is or must be.

A more plausible line of thought here has to do with the concept of forgiveness. What we cannot imagine, one might say, is that our imaginary Schindler could not eventually forgive himself if he has truly changed in the way that we have set up the example. That is, he is now not only caring but also without vanity, self-deception, unhopefulness, and so on. Under this description, if he lacks the capacity to forgive himself, either he possesses the vice of unforgivingness or he lacks the exceptional virtue of self-forgivingness. In the latter case, one might think that in extreme circumstances, the inability to forgive oneself is not a vice but the ability to do so is an exceptional virtue. Either way, however, there is a problem. In the event of the former, the breakdown is malignant, and in the latter, it is nonvicious. In neither case is it benign.

Although I have some reservations about the concept of forgiveness being given by someone who is not a victim, I admit that something like this might be the best way to think of this kind of case. Still, whether this ends the matter as to whether there can be benign breakdowns in response to former bad character is difficult to settle. It is true that I can be justifiably and deeply ashamed about something in my past without being ashamed about who I am at present. Nonetheless, it is not clear that if my shame is justifiable and deep enough regarding my past that I can make sense of looking at the present or the future with anything other than self-contempt, no matter what I am like now.

Consider the case of the serial killer Jeffrey Dahmer. Perhaps we cannot in the end imagine someone like this ever coming to review his life from a perspective of care that would even make possible integral breakdown of any sort over what he had done. That is, perhaps there is no coherent story that could be told about the evolution from this kind of malevolence to a deeply caring personality. That there could be such a story is anything but clear to me, but perhaps there is (though it would take some very extensive analysis to settle this issue). Let us simply assume that there could be for a moment. It is a further issue whether we could imagine anyone surviving such a change without integral breakdown. What would one have to be like to survive? More specifically, just what is the capacity for distancing oneself from having been such a depraved person within a personality that is now deeply caring, especially about one's past victims and their families, where the distancing allows one to survive? Because its psychological mechanism evades us, a clear picture of that capacity is difficult at best.

Perhaps it is the capacity to sever all psychological identification with one's past. This would certainly prevent integral breakdown due to having horrifying thoughts about what one has done to others. Yet it would make the concern for one's victims and their families like the concern for anyone's victims. Thoughts about their oppressor would be like thoughts about someone else; and being horrified about that would not be being horrified about oneself. What is difficult to believe is that such a capacity is consistent with both caring about others and an admirable attitude about oneself. In this regard, we sometimes console people who have accidentally caused great harm to others. We tell them that it was an accident, and we expect this to make a difference. Nevertheless, we do not expect it to make a difference too readily. If these thoughts make a difference too readily, we can only assume that there was not sufficient caring. There is a question, then, about what response is supposed to be indicative of both caring and the role of accident. We expect the kind of stress to be of the integral sort. If this is true, then the capacity for distance of the sort we are considering is not even to be found in cases of accidents, let alone in the more extreme cases like that of the serial killer. Think of the difference between learning that your neighbor has backed out of the driveway accidentally killing your child and that you have backed out of the driveway accidentally killing your child. It is one thing to help people get over the first kind of accident and quite another to help them get over the second. This I do not believe we would change about people. The reason, I think, is that we believe that to do so would be to change something good about them. I suspect we think that the only way to achieve such distancing is to make people less caring and that that would be bad. If this is true about accidents, surely it is also true about the horrible effects of one's former character.

What we need, then, is a way of conceptualizing a psychological state in which caring and thoughts about oneself are held together in a way that is horrifying. Moreover, if we are to avoid the conclusion that there can be benign breakdown as a response to former bad character, we need to imagine that the horror is integrally stressful but that something good about the agent's character prevents the breakdown. What I find difficult to imagine in some cases, especially where the former bad character is extreme, is what that good thing could be. If this is true, then the ability to recover from former bad character is not always a good thing. As to our soldier, we wish for a speedy recovery but understand that it cannot be immediate. This is in part because the failure was one of an exceptional virtue. As to Schindler, we cannot both admire him and expect that he is not pained by every thought of his vanity. Had he not exhibited exceptional virtues as well, our thoughts would be much different. As to Dahmer, recovery seemed unimaginable.

CHAPTER 3

Personal Love, Loyalty, and Benign Breakdown

The case for the possibility of benign breakdown does not rest on response to former bad character. Rather there are contexts in which integral breakdown is a response to what an agent has decided and done where what was done was not wrong. Some such cases involve breakdowns that are benign, or so I will argue.

I.

Consider the character Sophie from William Styron's novel *Sophie's Choice*[1] as an example of someone who was eventually destroyed by being forced to make a decision with which she could not live. The crucial decision, which involved a choice between the lives of her two children, Eva and Jan, was forced on her by a German officer when she arrived at one of the concentration camps during the Second World War. The usual procedure was for an officer to inspect the arrivals and assign them either to one line or another, leading either to the ovens or to the labor barracks and the possibility of life. On this occasion, however, the officer realizes that Sophie has perceived the implications of the decision and cruelly forces her to decide for herself which of the children will go to the barracks; otherwise, he will send them both to the line leading to the ovens and to certain death. Amid her agony, she finally succumbs to the situation, relinquishing her daughter to her death and saving her son for an uncertain future.

When placed within an understanding of her character at the time of the decision and her psychological development to that point and when traced through subsequent developments, the aftermath of Sophie's choice and the consequences of integral breakdown seem inevitable. As to her character at the point of her choice: it was neither impeccable nor without merit. She lacked exceptional courage but had already displayed a repulsion to anti-Semitism with a fearful participation in the Polish resistance. Most notable, however, was her loving commitment to her children, Eva and Jan. As to her psychology: it was burdened by shame for her anti-Semitic and professorial father, infected with some guilt over her lack of courage in the resistance, and filled with terror for the welfare of herself and her children.

The event that precipitated Sophie's dilemma involved her attempt to play on the Nazi officer's anti-Semitism as a means of gaining his favor and saving her children. Ignorant of his religious cynicism, she avows National Socialist affinities and claims that she and her children are not Jews at all but in reality are devoted Catholics. Pressed further about Jesus, the Redeemer, she professes the sincerity of her belief; and it is to this, as a test of her faith, that the Nazi officer challenges her with the awful choice. Her attempt to influence the officer, then, involved three things: it involved a disavowal of her hatred for anti-Semitism; it involved a religious appeal contrary to her actual contempt for Christianity (she believed that Christ had shown himself to be uncaring in allowing for the loss of her family and for the Nazi tragedy); and it forced a choice that might have been avoided.

With this understanding of her character and psychological development, how are we to understand the nature of the stress brought to bear on her by the choice? The hopes for the survival of one of her children have just been dashed, and it is *she* who must decide which is to live. It is not clear from the novel what her deliberations, if any, were. What is clear is that she faces a conflict of loyalties, both of which are among her categorical commitments. Both of her children innocently have complete trust in her commitment to them and cannot conceive of being abandoned by her. So it is not only her love for each of her children that is the source of tremendous integral stress; this would have been true even had the choice not been hers. Rather the stress is most poignant as it bears on the violation of trust between parent and child: if she chooses, she will violate the trust of one of her beloved children. Perhaps in this context, she was able to decide by virtue of the fact that she simply loved Jan more than Eva. Perhaps she reasoned that the boy had a better chance of survival in the camps than the girl. Or perhaps the "choice" was really not a choice at all but simply an act of hysteria. The novel itself does not reveal any answers here. However, if we assume that there was some sort of deliberative choice, it is difficult to see that the source of her stress was her thinking that she was doing something morally wrong. That would be to misdescribe the kind of stress she was under. In this regard, it is very important to understand that the thought that it was not wrong could offer her nothing in relief from the stress.

Subsequent to the choice, Sophie was separated from Jan and never learned after the war whether he had survived. Nevertheless, it was the hope of salvation for her son that allowed her to endure the camps. During this time, there is an episode that is very revealing of Sophie's character. Because of her linguistic skills and German appearance, she was moved to the commandant's house to serve as his secretary. While in this employment, resistance forces within the camp contacted her to seek help in stealing a radio from the commandant's house. Their thinking was that she could gain the commandant's trust by means of seduction and then put that trust to good use. Sophie expressed grave reservations because of the risk at which it would put her son. Nevertheless, she found herself gaining the confidence of the commandant. Her first thoughts, however, were not of making use of that trust for purposes of the resistance but for the liberation of her son. In this regard, she showed the commandant one of the anti-Semitic tracts written by her father as proof of her National Socialist sympathies in hopes that she could save both herself and her child. When this failed, she appealed to the commandant to place Jan within a special Nazi program for Polish children who had "Aryan" characteristics. This would at least ensure her son's survival. To this plea the commandant promised not only cooperation but that Sophie would be able to see her son one last time the next day. Filled with joy at this prospect, she headed down the stairs and saw the radio sought for by the resistance sitting unprotected and playing in the bedroom of the commandant's daughter. Haltingly she made her way into the bedroom with the intentions of taking the radio. She was caught, however, by the daughter before she could successfully remove the radio and was terrified that in an effort to help the resistance she had lost the chance to save her son. The novel does not reveal whether the daughter informed her father of Sophie's actions, but the scheduled meeting between herself and her son never took place.

After the war, Sophie finds herself in New York City and in love with another tragic figure, a Jewish intellectual named Nathan. Nathan's schizophrenia results in episodes that involve accusations against Sophie of infidelity to him and of cooperation in the Nazi conspiracy against the Jews while in the camps. Neither is true, but both have a devastating effect on Sophie, given her history and what she had to do for herself and others in the camps. When it is clear that Nathan has become a threat to both his life and hers, as well as to that of their friend, Stingo, Sophie leaves New York temporarily with Stingo in a desperate attempt to escape the tragic situation. Stingo genuinely loves Sophie and wants to marry her, have children, and live a normal happy life together. Sophie finds, however, that she must return to Nathan; she cannot abandon another loved one, nor can she hope for renewal in the real love that she perceives in Stingo. Her return, of course, comes with the inevitable suicide of the two lovers. At last, the integral stress of her life has reached its threshold.

II.

Clearly, the trauma of Sophie's choice initiated a psychological development, which, when exacerbated by further events, culminated in her complete destruction. It is this whole process that represents her integral breakdown. What does it say about her character? Reflection will reveal, I believe, that the only things that could have saved her were either bad character or good luck; nothing good could have been added to her character that would have saved her. I am not asserting that Sophie was a person with perfect character; she was not. Rather I am asserting that her vices were not causally relevant to her breakdown. If this is true, then the breakdown was neither malignant nor nonvicious but benign.

Consider first the possibility of malignancy. To say that the breakdown was malignant is to say that it was avoidable with the absence of a relevant vice. What, then, is the relevant vice? Some might assert that she viciously lacked the virtues of caring about other people, especially the Jews. Nathan in his madness would accuse her of this. Yet I cannot see that it is true that she lacked such caring or that having it makes any relevant difference. While in the camps, she risked the welfare of her son for the sake of the other prisoners when she thought she had his welfare secured. This testifies to enormous concern for others as well as to exceptional courage, contrary to what Sophie had thought herself to possess.

Perhaps, however, the point about caring for others is located elsewhere. The objection might be that had the strength of her respect and sympathy for others been morally sufficient, she could have found meaning in life despite what had happened to her and thus she could have avoided the tragic finale to her life. Here the thought is that even if life has spent itself in terms of personal love, the good person, the person with good character, can always find meaning in service to humanity. On this view, the breakdown was malignant because it expressed the absence of respect and sympathy for others.

The problem with this view is that it runs afoul of the psychological facts about respect and sympathy. Respect and sympathy do not in themselves give an agent reasons for living, although they do give an agent reasons for living one way rather than another. Respect and sympathy are agent-neutral dispositions. This means, first, that the respectful and sympathetic agent is dispositionally indifferent to the identities of those who are the intentional objects of respect and sympathy. Respect is sensitive to qualities of character, and sympathy is sensitive to the needs of others. Other qualities being equal, who has these qualities and needs is a matter of indifference. Second, it also means that the agent is dispositionally indifferent to the identities of those who are the agents of respect and sympathy. This is to say that the respectful and sympathetic agent is concerned that the dignity and needs of others be properly recognized and met by whomever is best placed to recognize such dignity or to meet such needs. It is only coincidentally, then, that respect and sympathy give us reasons for living one way rather than another. When we find in the course of our living that our actions have an impact on the dignity and needs of others, our respect and sympathy are triggered as motives to action. Otherwise, they are modes of caring consistent with empathy and inaction. This means that if we have the agent-neutral dispositions of respect and sympathy for others, we stand at the ready to let others secure the ends of respect and sympathy at any time other agents are better placed than ourselves to secure these ends. This is not true of the kinds of reasons that give us cause for living.

There is another difference as well. If the dignity and needs of others were completely met by others, requiring no action on the part of oneself, one could still be a perfectly respectful and sympathetic agent. This, like the previous feature, is not true of the sorts of things that give us reasons for living. If it is my commitment to excellence that centers my life, it is not enough that philosophy be done well but that I do it well. Moreover, even if philosophy were done perfectly well by everyone else, I would still have a reason for action, namely, my doing philosophy well. I cannot then be a person committed to excellence at what I do, unless I am dispositionally sensitive to the identity of the agent of excellence and unless I am engaged in activities that have excellence as their goal. Similarly, if my love for my loved ones is at the core of my reasons for living, then it is not enough that they receive personal love but that they receive it from me. Even if they were loved perfectly well by everyone else, I would still have reasons for action in regard to them, namely, expressing my love for them. Reasons of this sort are agent-centered in contrast to the agent-neutral reasons of respect and sympathy.

It does not follow, then, that if one does not have reasons for living that one is not a respectful and sympathetic agent or that if one is a respectful and sympathetic agent that one has reasons for living. For agent-neutral reasons for action do not have the conceptual features necessary in themselves for providing reasons for living. One would need to add something to respect and sympathy to derive reasons for living, namely, that what matters is that it is oneself rather than someone else who attends to the dignity and needs of others.

Two possibilities suggest themselves. First, one might believe that life has coincidentally placed one in a position to require one's unique qualities in the service of humanity for the rest of one's natural life. This borders on moral megalomania, hardly an admirable character trait. At any rate, it is anything but plausible to suggest that this was true of Sophie. It also has another problem that I will come to shortly.

Second, one might simply enjoy being in the service of others. Yet for this point to do the work of establishing the malignancy of Sophie's breakdown it must be shown that the incapacity for this kind of enjoyment is a vice. Here it is crucial to get a clear picture of what kind of enjoyment is at issue. It must be admitted, I think, that the inability to take a degree of delight in recognizing the dignity of others and in the sympathetic help with their needs is a vice. It is ludicrous, however, to think that it is a vice not to be able to take enough delight in others in these ways so that it gives one reasons for living in the face of numerous personal tragedies like Sophie's. Indeed, the security of this judgment seems stronger than any normative theory that would deny it. I cannot see, then, that either of these ways of adding to respect and sympathy will yield the conclusion that Sophie's breakdown was malignant.

Another possibility of malignancy has to do with the incapacity to act on principle. In this regard, there is a famous passage in Kant's *Groundwork of the Metaphysics of Morals* that comes to mind here. Kant is concerned with the moral worth of our actions, and he thinks that we have a duty never to commit suicide.[2] In most circumstances, fulfilling this duty is not much of an achievement since we have in reasonably favorable circumstances a natural inclination to go on living. For this reason, doing what duty requires seems to have no moral worth. Kant's point is not that one has to be miserable to be moral but that action has moral worth only to the degree to which it is motivated by principle. For him, a necessary condition for acting on principle involves the ability and willingness to act contrary to one's natural inclinations, and in this case, all of one's natural inclinations. To be fair or at least generous to Kant, it is not that one must in fact always act contrary to one's inclinations, but one must be willing to do so if that is necessary to doing the right thing. Imagining the person whose doing his duty in regard to the prohibition on suicide clearly does have moral worth, he says,

> When on the contrary, disappointments and hopeless misery have quite taken away the taste for life; when a wretched man, strong in soul and more angered at his fate than faint-hearted or cast down, longs for death and still preserves his life without loving it—not from inclination or fear but from duty; then indeed his maxim has moral content.[3]

On this view, it is a malignancy of character to lack the ability to act in the face of inclination that is contrary to doing one's duty. Indeed, this is the general form of failures of character on Kant's view. If one's respect for the moral law, one's ability to act on principle, is insufficient in its strength to allow one not simply to wish for the right thing but to will it, then one does not have a good will. Even if we fudge, and I do think that it is fudging, and allow Kant to say that the presence of a good will is consistent with the current inability to act in accordance with duty as long as the person is committed to doing everything psychologically possible to acquire that ability, failure of character is measured by the inability to act on principle in the face of contrary inclination.

On this view, Sophie's failure was malignant because she lacked the ability to preserve her life in the face of contrary inclination when moral principle requires that she not yield to this inclination. Or on the fudged view: her failure was malignant because she could not will to acquire the ability to live in the face of such contrary inclination.

There are two lines of attack on this attempt to show that Sophie's breakdown was malignant that are important to consider. The first is that the notion of acting on principle in its Kantian form is incoherent.[4] I believe that it is incoherent, but I will not argue that here. Kant was a brilliant philosopher who knew that he needed to posit the existence of "noumenal selves" to make sense of this notion of acting on principle and the view of agents embedded in his theory. That seems to me a sufficient reductio of his theory. I also believe that it is more difficult than some might think to tinker with the major concepts of his theory. Nevertheless, I leave it to those who think it promising to provide us with a coherent notion of acting on principle in this Kantian sense. For that they must not only provide a coherent notion of agency where one can act in the face of contrary inclination and where there is no other inclination as a motive. They must also show that the Kantian notion of agency makes sense of something much stronger. It is one thing to say that we can act in a particular circumstance in the face of contrary inclination and when no inclination motivates us. This is a hard thought in itself. It is quite another to say that we can live our lives in the face of such contrary inclination when no inclination motivates us. That is, it is one thing to say that we can act on principle; it is another to say that we can live on principle. In the case of Sophie, it is the latter that they must make coherent. I do not believe that coherence can be gained for either, but I will have much more to say about Kant in the following chapters.[5]

There is, however, another kind of problem that I want to emphasize relative to this notion of acting on principle. It is the problem of how a person could have the virtues of care as well as this kind of strength of will. What would it be to have the disposition to care about others only to the degree that no matter how many personal tragedies befall one, one can still find reasons for living? The notion of distancing oneself from one's feelings here is simply incompatible with having feelings that are deep enough to constitute the kind of caring we value so much in people. Cicero reports a view in De Amicitia with disapproval to the effect that one should only dispose oneself to intimacy with others in a way that is consistent with holding in mind that they might become enemies.[6] I cannot see that a concern for such protection is a reflection of strength. It seems more like cowardice, notwithstanding the fact that there is room for caution in forming friendships and other close personal relationships. Still the kind of caution of which Cicero disapproves is certainly incompatible with deep and intimate caring about others, as is the capacity to live in the face of contrary inclination when no inclination motivates. Moreover, it is important to note that while there is room for caution in forming close personal relationships, having these relationships consists precisely in overcoming such caution.[7] For those who think that this is simply a romanticized view of caring, as apparently Kant did, think of Sophie: was she simply "reveling in romanticism" when the thoughts of her children and the trauma of her losses exhausted her reserves for life?[8]

The issue, then, for this conception of malignancy is this: which is the character flaw, the inability to act on principle in this sense or the ability to care deeply and intimately about others? I cannot see the room for doubt that the latter is a virtue of the highest order. Moreover, this point also applies to the view previously considered in which respect and sympathy are thought of as sentiments. If we are to train our sentiments, assuming that we could, to be such that we are always to be able to survive any trauma and find our lives meaningful simply in terms of respect and sympathy for others, how can we do this and retain the capacity for deep and intimate personal love? Surely to stand guard on one's personal sentiments to this degree is to render them impotent; and this would be to destroy something good about us.[9]

If this is true, then we can transfer our conclusions about the breakdown not being malignant to its not being nonvicious either, insofar as respect, sympathy, and acting on principle are concerned. It is true, I believe, that the person capable of surviving the events of Sophie's life would be exceptional; but she would not be exceptionally virtuous. For the only way to make sense of training our sentiments and developing our capacity to live on principle in the way required here is really not by strengthening these capacities but by weakening or eliminating our capacities for personal love. Why? Because the capacity to give respect, sympathy, and acting on principle a place in one's life that eclipses the capacity for self-destruction as a result of trauma to deep personal love is not a capacity so much as an incapacity. For it involves not so much strengthening a person's respect and sympathy for others or the resolve to act in the face of contrary inclination as it does significantly weakening or removing these other motivational currents. Sophie would not be more respectful, more sympathetic, or more principled by the incapacity to be loving; she would simply be unloving. Yet to survive by being unloving is to survive by the lack of virtue. In this regard, love is like fuel in limited supply; it can be burned off, and one can die in the flames. We cannot change this about love; all we can do is either take our chances in this regard or abandon our commitment to being loving people. The result is that we cannot in this context, although we might in others, make sense of the virtues of exceptional respect, exceptional sympathy, and exceptional principledness. For this reason, we cannot make sense of her breakdown being nonvicious in regard to these factors.

Still, there might be other sources for the view that Sophie's breakdown was not benign. Perhaps instead of being as loving as I have depicted her, she was not loving enough. I have in mind here her relationship with Stingo and the possibility of future children. Sophie loved Stingo, though not in the way that he loved her. Why, then, if she were loving enough, could she not find meaning in his love and the prospects of having a loving relationship with a family that includes him? Does her suicide with Nathan not show that she was not loving enough? Or at the least, does it not show that she was not hopeful enough about the future possibilities of love for this to give her reasons for living? To be sure, loving in this way or having this kind of hopefulness might involve exceptional virtue, but this would show that the breakdown was nonvicious rather than benign.[10]

The response to this objection is that it overlooks the fact about love that it is a fuel in limited supply. The capacity to replace loved ones in one's life can only be limited. For at some point such a capacity slides into a kind of promiscuity incompatible with intimacy. This is a fact about human love and its phenomenal features. Love attaches to particular individuals and is incompatible with a disposition that allows either instant or endless substitution. No doubt we should eventually be able in most circumstances to find consolation on the loss of a loved one in the fact that there are others that we love. Nevertheless, if thoughts along these lines instantly dissolve our grief, it only reveals the lack of depth in our caring for the one lost rather than an abundance of it for those remaining. As to endless substitution, there is a point at which the capacity to replace lost loved ones can only be predicated on a sentiment that has been severely diminished.

Did Sophie, then, not love enough by not being able to detach herself from Nathan and their fate and attach herself to Stingo? Insofar as I can tell, Sophie's greatest virtue was that she never retreated from love. Her death with Nathan was itself an act of love; it was not a turning away from Stingo. What she knew was that her bountiful supply of love had come to its end. She knew that the tragedies of her life had exhausted her to the point that to go on without Nathan would lead nowhere but to her lovelessness. She also knew that going with Stingo would be to leave behind the one she loved more. Going with Stingo, then, would not have been loving more; it would only have been an act of desperation and a retreat from love. Moreover—and this is of the utmost importance—had she been a more loving person than she was, this would not have allowed her to survive; it would only have made the tragedies of her life more severe.

I close with one final attempt to reject the view that Sophie's breakdown was benign. It might be said that the impossibilities of combining love with unlimited strength are only empirical impossibilities. Nevertheless, the objection goes, it is logically possible to combine the virtues of love with unlimited strength, and this is all that is needed to avoid the view that there can be benign breakdowns. As long as we can have the thought that logically we could have been stronger and better, we are in a position to deny that these breakdowns are benign. Why? Because we can always say that we "could have" (logically) been better.

I believe that this objection fails on its own terms. For I do not believe that there is any sense to be made of its being "logically" possible to combine personal love with unlimited strength. However, this is not the line I want to pursue here. Rather I want to return to the earlier thoughts about wine and wine lovers. People who love wine in the truest sense, that is, people who love *wine,* are people who are profoundly attached to grapes—not to "logically possible" grapes but to those grapes that as a matter of fact can be cultivated and grown in the actual terra firma of the earth. To care in this way is to care for things fragile. So it is with those who admire lovers.

CHAPTER 4

Respect and Integral Breakdown

The previous two chapters have pursued the idea that benign integral breakdown can occur as a response to integral stress bearing on personal love as a mode of caring. Part of the argument there was that personal love cannot escape vulnerability to integral breakdown by alloying itself to the Kantian capacity to act on principle. So understood, personal love has an integral threshold that cannot be removed by adding other virtues. This is itself a criticism of the Kantian scheme. In the next several chapters, I want to pursue another line of thought, namely, that respect itself is best understood as a mode of caring with its own integral threshold and that it too is vulnerable to benign integral breakdown. The focus of my criticism is the idea of respect as a function of what Kantians call pure practical reason, a capacity purified of the psychological elements of desire and sentiment. I will say more about this shortly.

As a conceptual unit, chapters 4 through 6 reflect a division of labor. The work of chapter 4 is to isolate Kant's reasons for thinking that morality is inextricably linked to a certain view of ourselves and our worth as rational beings. As we will see, Kant had several reasons for thinking that morality is linked to the concept of pure practical reason. My purpose in this chapter is to give a summary of these reasons and to defuse some of them sufficiently to allow us to focus on two in particular. Critical are Kant's reasons for thinking that human dignity and the respect it is due are owed to the fact that we are rational beings of a certain sort. However, it is only in chapters 5 and 6 that the focus on human dignity and respect for it will become central. Chapter 5 will argue that our concept of human dignity involves the notion of vulnerability in ways for which Kantians cannot allow. Chapter 6 will argue that our conception of respect for others makes us vulnerable in ways that could not be true if our capacities for respecting others were a function of pure practical reason.

The current chapter, however, will first provide some clarification of what pure practical reason is supposed to be and then explore why Kantians think that the concept of moral responsibility and the concept of moral justification commit us to a conception of morality that requires pure practical reason. I will argue in each case that the conception of morality endorsed by Kant is tied to the notion of invulnerability and that we need not and, ultimately, do not, accept that conception. It is the requirement of invulnerability that ultimately drives the argument for pure practical reason, and we should not, after reflection on our values, be moved by that force.

I.

The first thing to do is to gain some clarification of what pure practical reason is supposed to be; then we can turn to arguments that morality requires it. In this regard, it is a feature of moral truths, assuming that there are such, that the recognition of them provides an agent with reasons for action. In this sense, to judge that one ought to do something is to recognize the normative force of a command or a prescription. Such judgments, then, involve imperatives that are action-guiding. But not all normative judgments and the imperatives associated with them are moral judgments. What, then, is the difference between a moral judgment that one ought to do x and a nonmoral judgment that one ought to do x? According to Kant, the difference is that moral judgments command categorically, and nonmoral judgments command hypothetically or contingently. This is easiest to see in the case of prohibitions. In the normal case, if I say to you that you should not see the film *Batman Forever*, I am not giving you moral advice or direction. In the normal case, I am simply asserting that it is not likely that the film will be worth your time, given your tastes and your desire for entertainment. The form of the judgment assumes two conditions: that you are interested in entertainment and that the film will not entertain you. But if the first condition obtains and the second does not, then, of course, you ought to see the film. That is, you ought in a clearly nonmoral sense to see the film.

But consider the prohibition on murder, clearly a moral prohibition. Are there similar conditions on such a prohibition? We do not say, "Do not murder, unless of course doing so will satisfy your tastes and desires," in the way that we say, "Do not see *Batman Forever,* unless of course you're into that sort of thing." In this sense, moral judgments seem to command categorically rather than contingently or hypothetically. This is why moral imperatives are categorical imperatives.[1]

But what kind of reasons could be provided to someone for categorical imperatives? According to Kant, they could not be reasons based on contingent desires or sentiments. Since desires and sentiments are contingent, they can provide the rational basis only for hypothetical, nonmoral imperatives. It is crucial then that the reasons for acting morally are such that they are provided by reason alone, that is, by reason purified of desire and sentiment. This means that reason alone must be able to motivate, a view that Kant held as a denial of David Hume's claim that reason is the mere servant of the passions. It is in this sense that practical reason must be pure on Kant's view. There must be some rational decision procedure for determining which acts are morally obligatory and which are not that does not require the conditions of desire and sentiment as their rational basis. The various formulations of the categorical imperative are supposed to provide this procedure, which any rational being can employ no matter what his or her desires and sentiments might be.

With this general understanding of the concept of pure practical reason, I want now to turn to the topic of why Kant thought it necessary to the concept of morality.[2]

II.

There are at least four routes to the idea of pure practical reason from a Kantian perspective, and they all begin with the concept of morality and proceed through a linking concept to the concept of pure practical reason. The linking concepts are the concept of responsibility, the concept of motivation, the concept of justification, and the concept of human dignity. I will call these linking concepts in the following sense: if A requires B in the sense that we cannot understand the concept of A without implying the concept of B, and if B requires C in the same sense, then B conceptually links A to C. Now, if we think of A as the concept of morality and C as the concept of pure practical reason, we are in a position to understand the structure of the Kantian argument. It is that some set of concepts, B, involving responsibility, motivation, justification, and human dignity, is conceptually implied in the concept of morality. This provides the link between A and B. Furthermore, we cannot understand the concepts included in B without implying C, the concept of pure practical reason. Thus, according to this argument, the concept of pure practical reason is implied in our conception of morality. Here I will not contest that any conception of morality implies some conception of responsibility, motivation, and justification. Nor will I argue for this. Neither will I argue that a conception of morality implies the concept of human dignity, though this is questionable. What I will be concerned to do is to argue that none of these concepts unproblematically links morality to pure practical reason.

Consider first the case of moral responsibility. Although Kant does not explicitly talk about responsibility in the *Groundwork of the Metaphysics of Morals*, the idea is lurking just near the surface of his discussion of other concepts. In the opening passages of the first chapter that focus on the concept of the good will as being good without qualification, Kant makes a distinction between gifts of nature and gifts of fortune. The thought is that many things that we find intrinsically good come to us accidentally as the result of the natural and social lotteries. Our genetic endowments provide many good things for us, things we value as ends, like our intelligence or bodily constitution. Similarly, the good fortune of being born into a family that has a certain level of wealth, that values education, and that is personally nurturing includes things we value as ends. Indeed, much of our personal happiness turns on our luck in these lotteries. Nevertheless, however good these things are as ends they are not good without qualification. For example, they can be extrinsically bad. The intelligence of the thief is instrumentally bad, and when happiness accompanies vice it makes the bad even worse because it is unjust that the vicious should prosper. More important, the goods of fortune and nature cannot be the grounds for our intrinsic worth even if they are part of the grounds for our happiness. Why? Because they are not things for which we are responsible. It is for this reason that the locus of goodness without qualification must be the will. Unless we are responsible for our value, it is not really *we* who are good without qualification. We cannot be responsible for our value unless we have a will that can determine itself in a way that is not simply the product of the causal interplay between accidents of nature and accidents of fortune. This power of determination is the power of pure practical reason, since a responsible will is one that determines its willings through self-generated laws of reason rather than through the "external sources" of the laws of nature, which operate in terms of desire and sentiment. To be responsible, then, we must enjoy a kind of invulnerability to our wills being determined by natural law through desire and sentiment. It is pure practical reason that provides for such responsibility by providing the invulnerability.

A bit later in the first chapter, Kant addresses the issue of moral motivation. His general thesis is that the good will is characterized by its motive, which is the sense of duty. Since only the person who is morally motivated has a good will, it becomes crucial to determine what the sense of duty as the moral motive really is. In this context, Kant distinguishes between motives that are practical and those that are pathological. The latter are motives that cannot be commanded, and the former are those that can. A child, for example, cannot be commanded to like his or her spinach, even where the command to eat the spinach makes sense as a means to a balanced diet. The taste for spinach, then, is pathological rather than practical in Kant's sense. Now, if we combine these thoughts with the previous ones regarding responsibility and the argument that it is the will that is the locus of unqualified value, we come to the conclusion that only motives that are practical rather than pathological can be moral motives. The will cannot be characterized by its motive unless the motive is internal to the will itself. Yet being motivated in this way is simply being motivated by the requirements of pure practical reason, not (at least essentially) by our natural and socially inherited motivations. Morality, then, requires motivation that stands outside the influences of natural law, and pure practical reason provides it, again, by providing a kind of invulnerability. Later, we will see how this applies to the concept of respect for persons.

The linking concept of justification functions a bit differently, and here it is the second chapter of the *Groundwork* that is crucial. The idea is something like this. Justifications that depend on a form of practicality that we might call prudence are in the end not fully justified. This is because the ends that justify the imperatives associated with them are pathologically determined. Hypothetical imperatives, then, do not simply differ from categorical imperatives in the kind of justification they provide. Rather they differ from categorical imperatives in that they do not provide justifications in any real sense at all. One is justified on Kant's view only if one's willings are self-determined, but if one's willings are ultimately determined by appeal to pathological ends, then one's willings are not justified; they are merely caused by external sources. This is true whether these pathological sources are those of narrow self-interest or more "altruistic" human sentiments such as are found in sympathy and personal love. For this reason, respect for others cannot be thought of as just another human sentiment on the Kantian view. Rather respect for self and others is pure practical reason itself, the will determining itself through the rational function of the categorical imperative and its procedures. As Barbara Herman says, unless justifications "go all the way down" to pure practical reason rather than stopping at some pathological end, there are no justifications in any real sense at all.[3] So once again we have a linking concept that requires that morality and pure practical reason are essentially intertwined in a way that implies invulnerability.

Finally, there is the linking concept of human dignity. In this regard, Kant is widely credited as the philosopher who gave us the insight that morality is specially connected to the idea that human beings are to be thought of and treated as ends, never merely as means. Moreover, the valuational status of the particular kinds of ends we are taken to be is to be understood in terms of the concept of dignity. After all, we might afford various things end status that we do not afford dignity status. What then would it be for something to have dignity status as an end as opposed to some other kind of end status? The answer is to be found in the kinds of valuational attitudes appropriate to different kinds of ends. The conceptual sequence seems to be the following: moral ends are ends worthy of respect; ends that are worthy of respect are only those that have dignity status; and only those ends that are capable of pure practical reason are worthy of dignity status. So once again, Kant is driven to the concept of pure practical reason by what he takes to be a central moral concept. Later, we will see more how this involves invulnerability.

III.

In the remainder of this chapter and in chapters 5 and 6, I want to turn a critical eye on each of these four concepts as they are found within the Kantian conception of morality. My primary concern is with the concepts of motivation and human dignity and their interrelationships. However, I do want to make some comments on the other two concepts of responsibility and justification. My goal is twofold. First, I want to show that Kantian arguments to the effect that morality and pure practical reason are linked through the concepts of responsibility and justification are flawed. They are flawed because they begin with a conception of morality that is open to question. In the case of responsibility, they assume that if we are to make sense of morality we not only must make sense of responsibility but responsibility of a certain sort. I will argue that this is questionable. In the case of justification, I will question the Kantian assumption that if we are to make sense of morality we must have a certain kind of guarantee of what morality requires. The second part of my goal is to show more precisely how Kantian conceptions of responsibility and justification are connected to invulnerability. In both aspects of this twofold goal, my aim is not to provide arguments that settle these matters once and for all. Rather, it is to say enough to allow us to proceed to the other linking concepts without worrying that we have ignored the issues of responsibility and justification.

Now, I want to turn to the issue of responsibility and the Kantian claim that through it morality and pure practical reason are inextricably linked.

The Kantians are right, I think, that some notion of free will is required by the concept of responsibility.[4] That notion must accommodate the capacity of a responsible agent to have acted otherwise in relevantly similar circumstances. Moreover, I believe that responsibility is a coherent concept. What I do not see is that we need the concept of pure practical reason as a basis for the concept of responsibility or that, at least on some interpretations, pure practical reason can provide that foundation. On one interpretation of Kant, the reasons for our actions must be sufficient for the occurrence of our actions if we are to be responsible for our actions. This is why pure practical reason just is free will on this interpretation of Kant. Yet this interpretation fails to accommodate the appropriate notion of free will. If responsibility requires that the responsible agent is free in the sense that one could have acted and willed otherwise in similar circumstances, then pure practical reason as a sufficient condition for determining the will violates this condition. For on this view, our reasons for our actions simply cause our actions.

However, someone might object that I have Kant wrong here. It might be said that Kant does not have the view that our reasons for our actions must be sufficient for our actions. Rather, on this interpretation, he might simply hold that they are necessary. On this view, cases of culpable wrongdoing are cases of acting contrary to one's reasons and cases of praiseworthy action are cases of acting on one's reasons. Free will, then, is the capacity either to act contrary to one's reasons for action or to act on them. Responsibility, though, is a more extensive concept than the concept of free will and includes having reasons for one's actions as well as the capacity to act either on or contrary to those reasons. Either way—whether one is culpable for wrongdoing or praiseworthy for right action—the concept of responsibility requires that one has reasons in the form of justification that would require doing the right thing.

The problem with this interpretation is that in itself it only links responsibility with justification. It does not link justification with pure practical reason. What is it that bars justification from having its foundation in something other than my will if my will is still free to act either on that justification or contrary to it? Of course, if the answer is that there is nothing that bars such a role for justification, then there is no link between justification and pure practical reason.

Someone might object, however, that I have the wrong picture of the relationship between motive and action. Suppose we distinguish between various elements relevant to understanding human action. First, there is the deliberative rationale for an action; second, there is the volition that precedes action as its cause; and, third, there is the action itself. With these distinctions we can construct two interpretations of Kant. According to the first interpretation, the relationship between motive and action is that the motive is to be understood in terms of the deliberative rationale and the volition where these are one and the same thing. The comments above indicate that there are problems with this first interpretation of Kant as being consistent with the appropriate notion of free will. On this view, having a motive just is believing that doing one thing rather than another is rationally justified, and the cause for any action just is the terminus of rational deliberation; there is no additional volitional antecedent.[5] On this view, an agent cannot willingly act contrary to what he or she believes as a result of rational deliberation.

On the second interpretation of Kant, the cause for action is to be understood as the deliberative rationale *plus* volition.[6] On this view, the content of the deliberative rationale is determined through the categorical imperative decision procedure. For example, deliberation in terms of the categorical imperative might yield the belief that one ought to keep one's promise. The agent then wills this action, the keeping of the promise, through a free act of volition, which causes the appropriate promise-keeping behavior. Now there may be nothing incoherent about this, but, even if there is not, this interpretation is not enough for the Kantian to establish the connection between responsibility and pure practical reason. What the Kantian must argue is that the second interpretation of Kant, or something quite like it, is required to make sense of moral responsibility where the deliberative rationale is spelled out in terms of pure practical reason. So the argument that the second interpretation of Kant is coherent is not an argument that it is necessary to the concept of moral responsibility.

To argue that the conception of action embedded in the second interpretation of Kant is necessary for responsibility would require that the deliberative rationale be interpreted in a certain way, namely, that only the deliberative procedure reflected in the categorical imperative is rational. Herman seems to think that Kant's view (with which she agrees) is that there are conceptual reasons for thinking that desires and sentiments in themselves cannot be motives.[7] On this view, a complex of desires, sentiments, and beliefs cannot in itself provide a deliberative rationale for anything, however much it might *cause* behavior. Nor can Herman and Kant allow that such a complex of desires, sentiments, and beliefs *plus* volition provides for a conception of motivation consistent with their notion of responsibility. To do so would be to jettison the need for pure practical reason. As I understand them, they want to argue that it is incoherent to assert that a person whose behavior has as its deliberative rationale a complex of desires, sentiments, and beliefs could be freely willed. But I do not see that there are any *special* problems with free volition here that do not apply when the deliberative rationale is provided by the categorical imperative. That is, the desire/sentiment view is no worse off regarding free will and responsibility than Kant's view, and is just as capable of accommodating the relevant notion of volition. Now if I am right about this, where is the problem with the desire/sentiment view providing for either motives or responsibility? Suppose a loving parent nurtures her child. Why deny that she is responsible for nurturing her child where it is her love that gives her a reason to do so and she has the volitional capacity either to act as her love prompts or to act contrary to it?

The answer might be that such a person is responsible but not responsible enough to be a moral agent. It is important to note, however, that even this answer gives away something the Kantian wanted to maintain as a basis for argument. If the Kantian allows that this agent is responsible but not morally responsible, the Kantian is allowing that a conception of practical deliberation based on desires and sentiments need not be attached to a mechanical conception of willing, a mere function of the natural and social lotteries.[8] What the Kantians must argue is that the deliberative rationale for *moral* responsibility must be understood in terms of pure practical reason and cannot be understood in terms of desires and sentiments. Our observations have established that the Kantian argument cannot be that only a pure practical reason standard of deliberative rationality can avoid a mechanical conception of willing. What, then, can motivate the argument for the pure practical reason standard and against the desire/sentiment standard regarding moral responsibility?

One possibility is an expanded notion of responsibility as far as the volitional component is concerned. On the view that practical deliberation is to be understood in terms of desires and sentiments, we are responsible for any particular act caused by our practical deliberations plus our volitions, because we can, on this view, voluntarily act contrary to our desires and sentiments. However, we cannot simply decide whether to have these components within our motivational set; for that we are not responsible. Thus we cannot be responsible for acting on standards of rationality that are not connected to whatever our desires and sentiments happen to be.

This is a very important point about the desire/sentiment conception of practical deliberation. The volitional variable spans the complete range of the agent's desires and sentiments, which allows for the possibility that an agent can always freely act contrary to rational deliberation. Yet this is to admit that the desire/sentiment standard of rationality allows for voluntary irrational action, which the appropriate notion of free will must accommodate. So the Kantians cannot reject the desire/sentiment standard on these grounds. Their real objection is that the desire/sentiment standard does not allow for important cases of voluntary *rational* action. It is this, say the Kantians, that only the pure practical reason standard of rationality can provide. Only this standard will make room for the thought that it is sometimes rational to do something that one does not want in any way to do, which is the idea of responsibility central to the Kantian argument.

Now it must be admitted that the desire/sentiment standard will not allow for this expanded notion of responsibility, and it is not a refutation of this objection to point out that whether one has the capacities for pure practical reason is itself something that is not open to volition. The fact is that the basic components of the desire/sentiment standard are pathologically determined in Kant's sense, but so are the components of pure practical reason, if we have them at all. Does this undermine Kant? I do not think so for the following reason. If a pure practical reason standard of rationality is coherent and true, there is no sense in which a person is prevented from having the motive to act rationally, even if a person has no desire or sentiment at all connected with that action. Now if we start with a conception of morality that sometimes requires us to do something that we in no sense want to do, then we need an interpretation of practical reason that cannot be satisfied by the desire/sentiment standard. However, if we start with a conception of human agency that requires a desire/sentiment standard of rationality, there cannot be any coherent version of practical reason that accommodates the idea that there are some acts that are rational no matter what our desires and sentiments happen to be. Therefore, the dispute over responsibility does not come down to a dispute over responsibility versus no responsibility. Rather it comes down to a dispute over different conceptions of responsibility, different conceptions of morality, and different conceptions of what we in fact are like. One cannot settle this kind of dispute simply by appealing to a contested feature of a favored conception, as the Kantians often do.

It might turn out that when we know enough about human agency, we will not be able to provide a rational defense of the concept of volition necessary for the appropriate notion of free will.[9] If that is true, then the concept of pure practical reason is dead, and so is, I believe, the concept of responsibility. Still, even if we can make sense of this notion of volition, it does not follow that we must construe responsibility in a way that requires the pure practical reason standard. A generally Aristotelian scheme, among others, is still open to us. Moreover, anyone who thinks that a desire/sentiment standard would not impose on us a significant share of responsibility has not thought very long and hard about what most of us are like in terms of our desires and sentiments.

It remains, then, to note that on the score of responsibility, Kantians are driven to a conception of practical reason that secures a special type of invulnerability. In order to be responsible in the Kantian sense, we must be invulnerable to the *excuse* that we are not the right sorts of beings to carry the burdens of morality. For this, we need *very* special powers. Settling the dispute about responsibility, however, is far beyond the scope of the present inquiry, and, in any event, would turn on the analysis of many other concepts. To say the least, it is not self-evident that the Kantians are right about responsibility. I must turn now to the subject of justification.

IV.

The Kantian argument for the justification linkage to pure practical reason is also flawed. If the thought is that acting on reasons is different from simply being caused to act in some mechanical fashion, non-Kantians can admit this while denying that rational justification must take the form of pure practical reason and the procedures of the categorical imperative. The comments on the concept of responsibility are enough to establish this. In this regard, what prevents someone from asserting that what justifies an action is that it is the sympathetic thing to do? One could believe this and believe that acting sympathetically is not simply a matter of motivational mechanics. The same can be said about a wide range of "natural inclinations" and their role in our lives.

Of course, there are other worries about the idea that something could be justified merely by appeal to the notion of sympathy. For any mature agent, the considered judgment that something is the sympathetic thing to do has already filtered through a number of other considerations. Among them is that the sympathetic thing to do is consistent with the demands of respect. It is interesting in this regard to note that insofar as one acts sympathetically toward another, one treats another as an end and not merely as a means.[10] The same is true of personal love, in any of its varieties. Indeed, personal love and sympathy for others are tempered by respect in the life of any admirable agent. The Kantians are right about this. Where they go wrong is not noticing well enough how the place of respect is also regulated by other sentiments. Again, for any mature agent, the considered judgment that something is the respectful thing to do has also already filtered through a number of other considerations. Among them is that the respectful thing to do is consistent with the demands of sympathy and personal love. So it is not true that sympathy can be a sole justifier, nor can personal love, but, then, neither can respect. Respect regulates and is regulated by these other concerns. This cannot be true on a conception of pure practical reason.

It is important here first to get clear on what cannot be true on a conception of pure practical reason and then on why it cannot be true. As to the first issue, consider a kind of concern among human beings that has the status of both being a regulator of other concerns and being regulated by other concerns. Parental love is a good example. A loving parent has a source of concern for another that regulates many aspects of the parent's life. For instance, parental love tends to negate the occurrence of neglect, either because of self-absorption or other factors. If there is too much neglect in a parent's life, this is a clear indication that the parent is not a loving parent. On the other hand, it is equally true that parental love is regulated by other concerns, like respect and sympathy for others, in the life of any mature parent. If there is too much favoring of one's own children to the neglect of others, then the parent is not a respectful and sympathetic agent. Parental love, then, provides a clear case of a kind of human concern that, on the one hand, functions as a regulator of other concerns and, on the other, is also regulated by other concerns. Can the concept of pure practical reason allow for this?

The answer is: only to a degree. Relative to personal love, Kantians can consistently assert that personal love is regulated by other concerns, especially the concerns of respect. Moreover, they can also maintain that relative to almost all other concerns an agent might have, personal love can and does function as a regulating concern. What they cannot maintain is that personal love, or any other human concern, can have a regulating function in relationship to respect. A similar analysis is true of sympathy, as well. On a Kantian view, there is no problem with sympathy for others both regulating other concerns and being regulated by them. Sympathy, for example, functions to prevent neglect of others and total absorption in loved ones. What sympathy cannot do on the Kantian view is have a regulating function vis-à-vis respect. Generalizing from this, we can say that respect is asymmetrical in its regulating function as it relates to all other motivational concerns.[11]

Now to the why question. Why cannot pure practical reason have a status that allows respect to be regulated by other concerns? The answer is that respect for others on the Kantian view has to be spelled out in terms of the procedures of pure practical reason. To respect oneself and others *just is* to govern one's deliberations regarding oneself and others by the rational procedures of the categorical imperative and its formulations. In this sense, respect, according to the Kantians, has to serve an integrating function that no other human concern can serve. Therefore, pure practical reason provides justification by taking into account everything there is to take into account, and there can be nothing external to that to regulate it. Since respect for self and others just is pure practical reason, respect regulates other concerns but cannot be regulated by them.

I do not believe that respect has this kind of asymmetrical regulative function in practical reason. This is not to deny that respect has a regulative function vis-à-vis friendship or any other sentiment. It seems sufficient to establish the regulating role of respect vis-à-vis friendship, for instance, to note the following point: when respect for self and others requires not favoring one's friend in cases of conflict, such a refusal to favor is not contrary to friendship on any plausible conception of friendship. So if I refuse to favor my friend because it would be unfair to a stranger to do so, I have not only acted respectfully; I have not violated the claims of friendship. Normatively, this is how the concept of respect regulates the concept of friendship.

Yet by parity of reasoning, the same can be said for the regulating function of friendship vis-à-vis respect. Again, note the point about friendship analogous to the previous one regarding respect: when friendship requires favoring a loved one over others in cases of conflict, as it surely sometimes must, this is not contrary to respect for others. Normatively, this thought has exactly the same structure as the previous thought about fairness regulating friendship. Why are we not in these cases thereby affording personal love in the form of friendship a regulating role versus respect for others? In the first case, respect for self and others puts limits on what one can justifiably do for one's loved ones. In the second case, personal love in the form of friendship puts limits on what one can do for other respectable people; and, normatively, this is how the concept of personal love in the form of friendship regulates the concept of respect for others.

It is not open to the Kantians to object that the standard for showing that respect could be regulated by friendship, or any other form of personal love, is that friendship sometimes requires one to act disrespectfully. For this would employ one standard for showing the regulating function of respect and another for showing the regulating function of friendship and personal love. There might, indeed, be conceptions of friendship that allow for disrespectful actions toward those worthy of respect. Yet what this shows is a conceptual scheme according to which friendship is not regulated by respect for others. It does not show that friendship, on an acceptable conceptual scheme, does not have a regulating function regarding the demands of respect for others.

If this is correct, then it is a mistake to think of respect as a function of pure practical reason. For considerations of respect do not have an asymmetrical relationship to the other regulating concerns within a rational agent's deliberative field. Moreover, it will not do here for the Kantian to assert that the categorical imperative *allows as permissible* actions that favor one's friends. We are thinking here of cases where one's actions would be contrary to friendship if one favored others over one's friend. Nor will it do to assert that it is respect for one's friend that carries the normative thought rather than love, because some such cases involve those where the respect for both the friend and the other person is equal. Thus, if these observations are correct, the Kantians have given us a false picture of the role of respect in the moral life and its role in moral justification.[12]

V.

The issue of motivation on the Kantian view cannot be understood independently of the issue of justification. To be morally motivated, according to Kant, is to be motivated to act on a certain form of justification expressed in the form of the categorical imperative and pure practical reason. Also, pure practical reason can have the function it does within justification only if respect has a different status within agency than other kinds of human concern. Friendship, parental love, sympathy, self-interest—all are concerns having a source in our affective capacities. As such, they operate on the conatus of desire through the affective mechanism and a form of consciousness that brings to bear on our agency a certain pathology. Respect, however, must be immune to this pathology, if we are to be rational creatures. This is why respect for oneself or another is not the triggering of an affective mechanism that is embedded in this pathological network. Rather, it operates in a purely cognitive way, which is why I say that respect just is pure practical reason on the Kantian view. The guiding thought here is that Kantian agency cannot depend on the contingencies of affective endowment for motivation, nor can it for justification.

There is some question about whether this is entirely consistent with what Kant says about moral feelings. Kant, as I understand him, does not maintain that feelings play no role in moral motivation. What he does maintain is that such feelings are generated by pure practical reason itself. The idea is something like the following.

First, distinguish roughly between the cognitive, affective, and conative capacities of an agent. My belief that 2 + 2 = 4 is a function of my cognitive faculties, at least in normal circumstances, as is my belief that I am now working at my computer. For Kant, it is important that my belief that it is my duty to keep my promises is also a function of my cognitive capacities. To be sure, such cognitive beliefs may factor in beliefs about the affective and conative capacities of myself and others, but this does not make my moral belief anything other than a function of my cognitive capacities. On Kant's view, it is one thing for me to *believe* that I am now working at my computer, another that I *believe that it is permissible* that I am now working at my computer, and still another that I *want* to be working at my computer. For Kant, it is crucial that the first two are products of one's cognitive capacities. This, after all, is what makes pure practical reason "pure" from the Kantian perspective.

The distinction between affective and conative capacities is well illustrated by the desire for a pleasurable experience. Pleasurable experience is made possible for us by our affective capacities. This is simply to assert that those things that are devoid of the capacities for consciousness of a certain sort are incapable of pleasure. Yet it is clear that we can experience pleasure and thus be in a certain affective state without that state being the object of desire. In fact, affective states usually precede the formation of most desires. For example, I first find the experience of tasting cognac pleasant and then come later to desire it.

Now, it is Kant's view that to be rational agents our cognitive capacities must govern our affective and conative capacities in the form of pure practical reason. Of course, there are those who question the crispness of these distinctions, especially any neat sorting out of cognitive capacities from the other capacities, but Kantians are in no position to raise such objections. It remains to be seen, then, how these distinctions bear on the role of moral feelings in moral motivation.

Moral feelings are essentially generated in conflict situations, involving a conflict between the cognitive dimension of moral belief—I ought not to do x—and the conative dimension—my wanting or desiring to do x. According to Kant, such a conflict for a rational being will generate a moral feeling. When one pictures oneself giving in to the conatus of contrary desire when duty is involved, one is filled with a feeling of self-contempt. Thoughts of oneself as anything less than a fully rational being, as having one's will determined without the purity of reason, are disgusting to a rational being, according to Kant. On the other hand, when one pictures oneself as acting on one's normative beliefs—beliefs generated by one's cognitive capacities—in the face of the conatus of contrary desire, one is filled with self-approval. This is the feeling of self-respect. Here thoughts of oneself as determining one's will in the face of nature is not unlike the feeling of the experience of the sublime, an experience of one part of ourselves being dwarfed by another part of ourselves, the cognitive dwarfing the affective and the conative.

According to Kant, this is a case of a feeling being generated by cognitive capacities in a purely rational way, but there are difficulties in seeing how this is a coherent cognitivist account. It seems to treat respect and its negative counterpart, self-contempt, as sentiments, and rather odd sentiments at that, namely, sentiments that have no pathology to them. Unless there is a prior sentiment intermediary between having the thought that I ought to do x and my wanting not to do x, there is no mechanism whereby the cognitive dimension alone can produce the feelings of self-respect and self-contempt. If there is such an intermediary, how can the will avoid an objectionable pathology? Kant's assertion, then, must be that this kind of sentiment is one that any rational being will have and that it is a purely rational sentiment. Yet it is anything but clear what a purely rational sentiment is. What can and must it mean to assert that a sentiment is purely rational? Three possibilities suggest themselves.

On the first alternative, a rational sentiment is a cognitive sentiment, a purely cognitive function. The problem is seeing how such a claim could be coherent. Feelings and sentiments may include a cognitive dimension, but even when they do they are not simply cognitive functions. If I am in the affective state of being afraid, for example, I have the belief that I am in danger; but certainly being in the affective state of fearing something comes to more than being in a cognitive state. With some exceptions, like general depression, most other affective states also carry some cognitive function in one way or another. Despite this fact, few would describe these states as simply cognitive states.[13]

On the second alternative, a rational sentiment is a sentiment caused or developed by reason alone, where reason is understood in purely cognitive terms. On this view, the cause of a dimension of one's subjectivity is not found in nature but in one's cognition understood non-naturally. Even ignoring the problems with understanding cognition in non-naturalistic terms,[14] this view suffers from a different kind of incoherence than the first alternative: namely, it fails to provide a coherent mechanism of production. How is it that the cognitive can create an affective foothold without some prior affective disposition to approve of oneself as a "rational being as such"? We understand how we can come to acquire a taste, for Italian food, say, even where there is no prior disposition toward the experience of it: latent capacities in myriad combination under prolonged exposure, and so on. Yet we do not and, I suspect, cannot think of acquired tastes as being cultivated out of thin air or out of materials completely nonaffective in their nature. Nor can I see any reason for thinking things any different when it comes to a proclivity for approving of ourselves under the descriptive terms of pure practical reason.

On the third alternative, a rational sentiment is an innate sentiment, rather than an acquired one, with a certain content, the disposition to approve of ourselves as rational beings as such. As a sentiment, it has one thing in common with all of our other dispositions: it is an affective capacity rather than a purely cognitive one. Yet, unlike other desires and sentiments, even others that might be innate, it responds only to cognitive prompts of a certain sort and is indifferent to all others. Its innateness avoids the coherence problem of the second alternative, but it is the content-sensitivity of the sentiment that makes it purely rational and secures immunity from an objectionable pathology.

Now let us suppose that this is a coherent view as far as things stand at the moment. There remains the difficult question regarding what the forces of nature would have to be such that a sentiment of this sort would evolve through natural selection in a manner that would bridge the gap between the rational and the nonrational in just the right way. Our genetic endowment, I understand, is much the same as it was ten thousand years ago at the end of the dominance of hunting/gathering societies. With this in mind, perhaps there is a "just so" story to tell here about the survival value of a mechanism held to be so central to human psychology in such an environment, but it does not leap readily to mind. What is difficult to see is how the selective process in such an environment would not have selected *against* such a psychology by selecting *for* more localized and pathological sentiments. In this regard, Kant might have thought that the noumenal world works outside the evolutionary process. It is difficult, however, to see how we can find philosophical illumination in such esoterica.

On this topic, contemporary Kantians seem to have little to say, and one cannot help but feel that there is a bit too much a priori philosophy of mind going on. One should worry, I believe, when one's conception of morality turns on concepts appropriate to other areas of philosophical inquiry and where those concepts are deeply problematic. The problem here is the drive to find a conception of agency immune to pathological influence.

Motivating that drive is a special kind of invulnerability sought for moral justification on the pure practical reason standard. It is the invulnerability to moral mistake, a decision procedure that guarantees moral *infallibility*. On this conception of morality, if we make a moral mistake about what it is that we ought to do it must be such that it could have been prevented with clearer thinking. Now, it must be admitted that any conceptual scheme that does not encourage the clearest thinking possible is deeply flawed. However, it is another thing altogether to begin with a criterion for evaluating conceptual schemes that a scheme is to be rejected if its conception of practical reason does not include a guarantee of infallibility. Why should we start with the view that morality is possible only if there is some decision procedure that guarantees errorless results if properly employed? When we have cared about others in all the ways possible for us—when we have factored in our respect for others, our sympathy for others, and our love for others—and when we have been as clear-headed as possible, might mistake still be possible? Might philosophical reflection reveal that what we value most in ourselves and others renders us vulnerable even to mistake? If so, then there is no reason why we should be driven by a conception of morality that requires infallibility. With these and other issues in mind, I turn to the concept of human dignity.

CHAPTER 5

Dignity, Kant, and Pure Practical Reason

I.

According to Pauline Christianity, we cannot enter the Kingdom of Heaven without grace; and without dignity, according to Kant, we cannot enter the Kingdom of Ends and become members of the moral community. Understanding the Kantian conception of dignity, then, is crucial to understanding the Kantian conception of morality. In the next two chapters, I want first to clarify the Kantian conception of human dignity and its relationship to the concept of pure practical reason. I then want to criticize that conception in the light of an alternative conception, where I will argue that the Kantian conception of human dignity fails its own criterion of unqualified value. It fails, I will argue, by not being able to give adequate place to the fact that our vulnerability to integral breakdown is essential to what gives us our dignity.

II.

It will be helpful in understanding the Kantian conception of human dignity to make a distinction between moral agents and moral subjects. Moral agents are those beings who are responsible for carrying out the imperatives of morality and for fulfilling the obligations imposed by it. As I understand Kant, all and only rational beings are moral agents. This means that God and normal human beings are moral agents, since they are rational beings, but that dogs and cats and such are not moral agents, since they are not rational beings. Thus a dispute over whether someone is a moral agent is a dispute over whether that someone is a rational being. As long as we do not presuppose what rationality comes to, this seems correct. One way, then, that one can have citizenship in the moral community is by qualifying as a moral agent vis-à-vis the possession of rationality.

Moral subjects, on the other hand, are those beings who are due intrinsic moral concern and, as such, are the direct beneficiaries of morality. My understanding of Kant is that only but not all rational beings are moral subjects in this sense. God is not a moral subject, despite the fact that He is rational. To be a moral subject, one must be susceptible to the laws of cause and effect, to the laws of nature; specifically, one must be susceptible to the actions of others as cause to effect, and God is not. God, then, does not stand within the causal nexus vulnerable to its effects; He transcends the mechanisms of nature, affecting it but not being affected by it; and He is untouched by the actions of others. Utterly transcendent of nature in this sense, He stands to benefit neither from nature nor from morality. Yet He is a moral agent in relationship to whom we and all other rational beings are moral beneficiaries. God's status within the moral community, then, is solely that of a moral agent; and He is, of course, its most dignified member.

Yet to say that God is the most dignified member of the moral community is to make a limited claim about God's *value*. In one sense God has no more value than any other member of the moral community. This follows from the kind of value dignity has. In this regard, Herman says, "The person with a good will is of no greater value than one with an ordinary will; she has no greater amount of dignity. As rational agents, we each have the capacity to bring our wills into conformity with the principle of good willing, and so each has all the dignity there is to have." She continues further on the same page, "As the final end of rational willing, rational nature as value is both absolute and nonscalar. It is absolute in the sense that there is no other kind of value or goodness for whose sake rational nature can count as a means. It is nonscalar in the sense that (1) it is not the highest value on a single inclusive scale of value, and (2) it is not additive: more instantiations of rational nature do not enhance the value content of the world, and more instances of respect for rational nature do not move anything or anyone along a scale of dignity. There is no such scale."[1]

Thomas Hill, who arguably takes the Kantian conception of dignity more seriously than any other contemporary moralist, says, "dignity cannot morally or reasonably be exchanged for anything of greater value, whether the value is dignity or price. One cannot, then, trade off dignity of humanity in one person in order to honor a greater dignity in two, ten, or a thousand persons."[2]

The result is that if dignity does not come in quantities and is non-scalar, then God cannot have more dignity than the meanest scoundrel if the meanest scoundrel has any dignity at all. As offensive as this kind of radical egalitarianism might be to many religious persons, they might find some solace in the fact that there is a sense in which God is nonetheless more dignified than humans, even on Kantian theological standards. God's dignity is "purer" than that of humans, which is to say that God's reason, His dignity-conferring quality, is less soiled by values of the empirical self and less vulnerable to the powers of cause and effect than is human reason. Granted, this does not, on the Kantian view, make God of greater value than the meanest scoundrel, but it does make Him "purer." It is in this sense that God is the most dignified member of the moral community, but as a moral agent, not as a moral subject.

Also excluded as moral subjects are lower animals. That is, nonhuman animals are not due intrinsic moral concern and, as such, are not direct beneficiaries of it. This does not mean that we do not have obligations to nonrational animals. We do. But when we do, these obligations derive from our obligations to ourselves and others as rational beings. In the first place, I can affect a rational being by virtue of his or her relationship to a nonrational being: by abusing your cat, I do something to you. In the second place, I can affect my own character and its bearing on other rational beings by developing uncaring traits toward animals: by abusing your cat, I feed the general lust for violence of which you might become a victim. Without these connections to rational beings, however, lower animals would in no sense have any moral standing. Why? Because they have no dignity; they lack rationality.

This leaves humanity as the class of moral subjects, which gives us double membership in the Kingdom of Ends.[3] On the one hand, as moral agents we are responsible for moral directives and have the obligations of such a role in membership, where the relevant qualification for this role is our rationality. On the other hand, as moral subjects we qualify for moral concern not simply by virtue of our rationality but also by virtue of the fact that we can be affected by the actions of others. It is in this sense that we are moral beneficiaries. Nevertheless, if we lacked rationality, the fact that we could be affected by the actions of others would be of no moral importance. This is because if we lacked rationality we would have no dignity and would not be worthy of the concern of others.

We are, then, both like and unlike both God and nonrational animals. Like God, we are rational beings, but unlike Him, we are vulnerable to the laws of cause and effect and the actions of others. As to nonrational animals: like them, we are vulnerable to the laws of cause and effect and the actions of others; but unlike them, we are rational. What is very important for our purposes at this point is that it is only in terms of the fact that we are like God that our vulnerability has any moral significance. So, on the one hand, we are creatures that have one foot, so to speak, firmly situated in nature and its causal network. On the other hand, we are creatures transcendent of such a network in virtue of our rationality. Yet note that it is the transcendent part *alone* that provides the value that motivates the concern, and it is the value of the transcendence of rationality that is the value of our dignity. Indeed, according to Kant, it is the failure of any nontranscendent, naturalistic conception of practical reason to provide us with an adequate account of the value of dignity that rules out any naturalistic conception of morality.

Our dignity, according to the Kantian conception, is systematically eliminated without transcendence. That we are responsible for our actions and willings is a part of our dignity; but, as we have seen, without rationality that transcends all our desires and sentiments, according to Kant, there cannot be such responsibility. That we are capable of a certain kind of motivation is a part of the value of our dignity; but, again, without transcendent rationality, we cannot, according to Kant, be so motivated. Finally, that we are capable of justifying our actions by appeal to reasons is a part of our dignity; but, here too, without transcendent rationality, there can be no such justification. Therefore, on the Kantian conception of human dignity, transcendence is crucial to any dignity-conferring quality.

III.

In this regard, it is important to keep in mind that any conceptual scheme that places a value on transcendence implies a hierarchy of both transcending and transcended qualities, which can include both powers and values. According to Christianity, for example, the spiritual/worldly distinction is one that ranks spirituality above worldly concerns both as a value and as a power: the good forces of God and spirituality will prevail over the evil forces of the world in the end. Here spirituality is the transcending quality, and worldly concern, the transcended. The relevant duality for Kant is one involving rationality and nature as transcending and transcended qualities, and the hierarchy involves both values and powers. So we are back to issues of strength and quality of character, where both strength and quality are features of a transcendent value.

The value of dignity, according to Kant, is related to the kind of value a good will has, namely, the value of being good without qualification. He thinks we are committed to the following propositions if we are committed to the concept of morality:

1. Necessarily, there is something that is good without qualification;
2. Necessarily, the good will is good without qualification; and,
3. Necessarily, the good will alone is good without qualification.[4]

The criteria for being good without qualification can be extracted from the text,[5] and they seem to be the following: for any x, x is good without qualification, if and only if, x is

a. intrinsically good,
b. never extrinsically bad,
c. the most fundamental good, and
d. good independent of its consequences.

Something is intrinsically good if it is valuable as an end, which does not rule out that something could be both intrinsically good and instrumentally good. However, to the extent that the value of a thing depends on its instrumentality, its value is conditional on the value of some external end. Thus instrumental value never adds anything to unconditional value.

Something can be extrinsically bad in at least three ways, all of which are either explicit or implicit in what Kant says. First, something can be extrinsically bad by being an effective means to a bad end. A hammer, for example, can make an effective murder weapon. Second, something can be extrinsically bad by being an ineffective means to a good end. In this regard, a knife does not make a very good toy for an infant. Finally, something can be extrinsically bad by decreasing the value of that to which it is added. Cream might enhance the flavor of coffee, but it will ruin a Chardonnay.

Something is a fundamental good relative to another good if it is necessary for the value of that other good. Some people, for example, believe that sex is good only if it is accompanied by love. On this view, love is a fundamental good in relationship to the good of sex. Something is the *most* fundamental good if it is necessary for the value of any other good but its value is not dependent on the value of anything else. Thus the concept of the most fundamental good includes a completeness criterion, namely, that nothing can be added to a most fundamental good to make that good any better. Kant believes that only the good will is fundamental in this sense.

Finally, something could be good independent of its consequences in two ways. First, something could be good independent of any bad effects traceable to it. Someone might believe, for example, that cigarettes are good even if they do shorten lives and cause misery. Second, something could be good because it has intrinsic value and no bad effects can be traceable to it. Consistency requires the second as a reading of Kant, I believe. For the first is inconsistent with the requirement that whatever is good without qualification cannot be extrinsically bad. In fact, this criterion can be read as a special application of the requirement that to be an unqualified good something cannot be either a bad means to a good end or a good means to a bad end.

According to Kant, only the value we afford to a good will can meet all these conditions. What is that value? It is the power of transcendent reason to determine the will independent of natural desire. Thus, for Kant, strength and quality merge in the single factor of transcendent rationality, the rationality of pure practical reason. However, one can have dignity without having a good will, but to have dignity one must have the power of pure practical reason whether one uses it or not. Thus the concept of human dignity is attached to the concept of transcendent rationality through the concept of the good will: having dignity is having the capacity for a good will, and having the capacity for a good will is having the capacity for determining one's will through the transcendent power of rationality independent of natural desire. It is dignity in this sense, according to Kant, that is the intentional object of respect for persons.

IV.

Now to see in what sense such transcendence implies immunity from vulnerability to integral breakdown. Kant is right, I believe, that we value rationality, on some interpretation, as an end, not just as a means. Yet is it true that the value we place on persons, even their rationality, is connected to the concept of unqualified value? Even if it is, does transcendent rationality meet the criteria? I am not confident of an answer to the first question, though I am inclined to a negative one, but I am much more confident that a negative response to the second is correct.

A negative answer to the first question is correct if there is no considered set of admirable qualities that will in combination meet all the criteria for being good without qualification. Let me suggest reasons for suspecting this to be true. Although one might attempt to undermine the concept of unqualified value by arguing that there is no logically consistent set of criteria to specify the concept, this is not what I have in mind. I see no reason for asserting that even if there were something that did satisfy the criteria it would still have only qualified value. Rather, what I have in mind is the objection that for any considered set of qualities at least one of the criteria will be unsatisfied. By a "considered set" I mean a set of qualities about which a considered philosophical judgment has been made about its being an admirable set of qualities.[6]

Now why the doubts that there can be such a set? It seems to me that it might be true, as a matter of fact, that, rationality notwithstanding, there is no admirable trait—no trait that we in fact admire on consideration—that when psychologically instantiated in humans does not have a cost in terms of other admirable traits. One possibility is that there is no such admirable trait that when psychologically instantiated does not carry with it the instantiation of some vice. This would violate Kant's fourth criterion of unqualified value, namely, that to be unqualifiedly good something must be good independent of its consequences. Another possibility is that there is no admirable trait that when psychologically instantiated does not preclude the instantiation of some other equally admirable trait. This would seem to violate the combined effect of Kant's last three criteria. For it is one feature of goodness without qualification on these criteria that not only does it impart value to things that otherwise would lack value, it never precludes anything good. If this is true, it is a mistake of no small order to attach the concept of dignity to unqualified value, for it is to attach human dignity to a fiction.[7] This in itself should lead us to search for an alternative conception of human dignity. For we should not jettison the concept of human dignity until we have considered it differently and found it wanting even then.

V.

Putting these doubts aside for the moment, however, we come to the second question: does the will as motivated by transcendent rationality meet the criteria of unqualified value? There are, I believe, three major features of transcendent rationality as described by Kant that make it seem to meet the criteria of unqualified value. The first is that it is a non-egoistic form of consciousness. Kant's intuition here that we would not admire someone whose only thoughts were ultimately for him- or herself is surely correct, although it does not follow from this that pure practical reason is the only way of making sense of the denial of egoism. Anyone who has a governing intrinsic interest in the interests of others is nonegoistic, and this is true on Aristotelian and many other naturalistic accounts of human motivation.

A second feature is that transcendent rationality can never lead one to an erroneous moral judgment, whereas every other motive can. The thought is that when one makes a mistake about what one ought morally to do such a mistake can never be traced to the good will, to pure practical reason, but to some other countervening influence. This is why bad consequences are never traceable to a good will. Being motivated to do what transcendent rationality requires can never in itself lead one to act contrary to what transcendent rationality requires. What could be clearer than that?

There are two problems with this view, I think. First, it is not clear that we should say that all other motives can lead us to do that which is wrong. Take sympathy, for example, one of Kant's whipping posts. Can sympathy ever lead us to do the wrong thing? I admit that there is some initial plausibility in this line of thought. I remember years ago working with burn patients where it was necessary to remove burned skin to avoid infection. This was often a very difficult task for those who were sympathetic to the plight of the patients in anticipation of their pain. Some assigned to this unpleasant work labored very slowly and deliberately removing the skin, and they could not bring themselves to get on with it as expeditiously as possible. Of course, their approach only made things worse for the patients. One might say that their sympathy led them to do the wrong thing. But as plausible as this sounds initially, I believe that it is mistaken. In the end the people who took it on themselves to be as efficient as possible under these circumstances were those whose sympathy initially prevented them from doing just this. The initial reluctance to proceed expeditiously was taken as a conscious task to overcome for the sake of the patients. What they lacked initially, then, was not some extrasympathetic motive but informed or mature sympathy. Had they not been able to proceed when adequately informed about proper treatment and the prospects of the patients, they would have been wanting in sympathy itself, not some other virtue.

There are, of course, cases where sympathy or personal love will not guide one morally, either because they do not apply or because there are other relevant variables. Yet these are not cases of sympathy or love leading one to do the wrong thing, but cases of sympathy and love not in themselves being able to give sufficient direction. In fairness to Kant, however, it does follow from this that neither sympathy nor personal love is of unqualified value. On the other hand, this qualified value of sympathy and personal love does not indicate that they lead to the abuse and mistreatment of others either. Rather, such mistreatment is more plausibly traceable to the absence of other kinds of concern for others. My loving my child does not lead me to mistreat others; my lack of respect for other children does. The evidence for this is that we do not try to remove the love to prevent such behavior but to add respect. Still this shows that sympathy and personal love are not unqualifiedly good because something can be added to a will that is influenced by them to make that will better, namely, respect.

This brings us to the second problem with Kant's claim that the good will can never be the source of moral failure. He assumes a view of the good will that identifies it with transcendent but practical rationality. I have already given reasons for doubting this when I argued that personal love and sympathy have regulating roles vis-à-vis respect for others in practical reason. Recall that our respect for others does not always require us to favor others over our loved ones and that our love for our loved ones does not always allow it, even where respect is held constant. This is contrary to a view that identifies respect for others with pure practical reason. In one sense, then, Kant is right: the motive to do the right thing cannot in itself ever lead one to do the wrong thing. Nevertheless, there are good reasons for doubting that the motive to do the right thing should be understood as simply a function of respect where respect is simply a function of transcendent but practical rationality.

Finally, we come to the third feature that leads Kant to think that transcendent but practical rationality is good without qualification, namely, its nonpathological nature.

VI.

The issue of pathology is central to the Kantian conception of agency. The central point is this: unless a subject, a conscious being, has some capacity for action that transcends pathological influence, then that sub-ject is not an agent. Moreover, the peculiar value of dignity, whether human or nonhuman, attaches to agency, not some other feature of con-sciousness. It is only because these other features of consciousness attach to agency that they matter, when they matter. For Kant, the transcending feature of consciousness requisite for agency is rationality. He calls it pure practical reason. It is practical because it directs action, and it is pure because it transcends the causal nexus that prevents agency. Nothing could be less vulnerable than that. The net result is a conception of human dignity that is attached to invulnerability. I will argue that this cannot be correct, especially when it comes to what we value in human agency.

Some might object that this is not a correct reading of Kant, and oth-ers that it is simply an artifact of his conception of morality rather than anything essential to it. Later, I will consider some of these thoughts. Now, however, I want to show just how wide of the mark this concep-tion of human dignity really is. If I am right, the Kantian conceptual scheme is not nearly as sensitive to ordinary moral consciousness as it should be or as many have thought it to be.

I begin with a concession to the Kantian scheme. It seems to me that it is a part of our conception of human dignity—one that is very diffi-cult to give up—that humans are not simply very sophisticated machines. Some non-Kantians will certainly disagree with this, but my argument here is not with them but is limited to an exchange with the Kantians. So one extreme view of agency and dignity that I do not find compat-ible with a deeply held value is a view that effectively reduces us to machines—complex machines, even conscious machines, but machines nonetheless. However, if honest and intelligent inquiry reveals that we are such machines, as philosophers who are concerned with the truth of the matter, we should be willing to accept the facts and either alter our conception of human dignity or give up the concept entirely.

Still it is one thing to think of human agency as not reducible to some mechanical model and quite another to think of it as invulnerable to cause and effect. There is a great deal of room between having some control over one's life, even some transcendence in some important sense, and the kind of transcendence afforded to rationality on Kant's view. Making coherent sense of either conception of transcendence is a problem, and a considerable one, for an adequate philosophy of mind. This, however, is not the problem I want to focus on here. My focus here is on the coherence of attaching value to a conception of agency that employs the Kantian conception of transcendence even in the event that it can be made coherent. What I want to question is what is so valuable about agency so construed.

We have, then, two extremes: machinelike lower animal consciousness without agency and Godlike consciousness with complete invulnerability and ideal agency. The former does not include the kind of dignity I would describe as rich enough to apply to humans,[8] but then neither does the latter. Moreover, I believe this latter point is true on almost everyone's considered judgment. Not only do I believe that agency without the possibility of vulnerability is incoherent, I believe that the value we place on agency is in part a function of the kind and degree of vulnerability agency is subject to. Were we ideal agents on Kant's view, we would not be subject to vulnerability at all. In this regard, there is nothing in Nietzsche's view concerning power that remotely places so much emphasis on strength as is found in this central feature of Kant's conception of morality.[9] My claim here is that on reflection we do not put such an emphasis on strength in our assessment of character and human dignity.

It is puzzling what is supposed to be so admirable about omnipotence, even when employed in the service of good ends. True, such strength may be extremely beneficial, but as Kant points out, when speaking of dignity we are not speaking of the beneficial. What, then, is so admirable about God and His invulnerability to the laws of nature? In short, what is so admirable about his transcendence? Finally, what is so dignified about it? Everything that is in any sense possible is equally and infinitely easy for God; that is what it is to be omnipotent. It should not be thought that among those feats that are logically possible some are a bit more difficult than others but nonetheless possible for an omnipotent being. How could the notion of degree enter into the concept here? God can do anything with infinitely more ease than it takes for any of us to blink our eyes. Consequently, we should not think that we admire God for accomplishing extremely difficult tasks. Nothing is difficult for God. Yet without the concept of difficulty, where is either the concept of agency or the concept of dignity? Dignity seems to be essentially caught up with the capacity to bear up under difficult circumstances. Yet on the Kantian view of practical rationality and human dignity, we have dignity to the extent to which we are like God, the purely rational being immune to the laws of cause and effect. Something has surely gone wrong somewhere.

Moreover, it seems that the concept of dignity is not only caught up with the notion of overcoming difficulties but also with the more formidable concept of running the risk of insurmountable difficulties. Indeed, it seems that we generally think of dignity as attaching to a person who strives to live a good life in the face of difficulties some of which pose the threat of ruin. True, Hitler strove for a life that faced difficulties that posed the chance for ruin to a rather high and accurate degree, but the kind of life he strove for was not one that we could judge worthy of pursuit. The contemptible quality of his commitments disqualified his willingness to face difficulties from conferring dignity on his life. On the other hand, a life that faces only the possibility of trivial difficulties seems at most fortunate (and there is some doubt even about that), but it is hardly one that faces the conditions requisite for dignity. For example, if the only difficulties I could possibly anticipate in my life were those involving having to give up, say, a minor interest in eating chocolate, I could hardly be a person with much in the way of dignity. This would be true no matter what my giving up chocolate would make possible. Let me be clear here that I do not mean that one has to be constantly struggling to have dignity. Instead, what I mean is that dignity requires an environment in which an agent anticipates real dangers to significant commitments and stands ready to face those dangers without abandoning those commitments. The life of utter safety regarding all but one's minor interests is not an environment in which this is possible or one in which dignity can have a place. For this reason, human agents are better models for ideal agency than the God of Kant or the Apostle Paul. Dignity, then, requires reference to an effort at living a good life and a willingness to face difficulties of a substantial sort.[10] But what sort is that?

Here it will be helpful to recur to the concept of integrity and what makes integrity possible. Recall that it is one's categorical commitments that are the center of one's integrity. Thus the kind of danger relevant to dignity is the danger that threatens to fracture the core of a person's life. This is the threat of integral stress. Without the concept of integral stress, a conceptual scheme is unable to provide the context in which there is danger of the sort relevant to the possibility of dignity. Since God is immune to such stress—since there is no possible context in which He could face the kind of danger that would produce such stress—how could the concept of dignity apply to Him?[11] Also, if what confers dignity on us is a feature of our agency that is immune to any pathology and that simply transcends the contexts of integral stress, how is it that that feature can confer dignity? I simply do not see it.

Here it is important to note that the concept of acting in the face of contrary inclination will not do the relevant work for the Kantian. It might be thought that Kant's views about the sense of duty requiring one to be willing to act in the face of contrary inclination should duty require it accommodates everything I have said thus far about dignity. Yet even ignoring the problem that contrary inclination does not arise for God, whose dignity is purer if not more valuable than human dignity, this objection misses the point. There is no way that our dignity-conferring capacities, to the extent to which we have them on the Kantian understanding of those capacities, can render us vulnerable.

If our being respectful agents is what confers dignity on us, and if being respectful is what Kant says it is, then it is difficult to see how our capacities for respect could ever render us vulnerable to the dangers of integral stress. How could the source of integral breakdown ever be located in our capacities for respecting ourselves and others? Integral breakdown would always have to be found in some other, pathological feature of our psychology. On the other hand, if we think of our vulnerability to integral stress as having its source in our deepest commitments—commitments that include respect for ourselves and others—we thereby afford intrinsic value to that which does not transcend the pathological features of our psychology in the way appropriate to Kant's argument concerning unqualified value. Thus there seems to be a dilemma. Kant could deny that respect for self and others has a pathology with a limitation threshold regarding integral stress, in which case he would inherit the difficult problem of reconciling our transcending powers with the concept of dignity reasonably understood. Or he could accept the pathological nature of respect and its intrinsic value, in which case he would have to abandon some of his claims about the unqualified value of the good will as he understands it. More specifically, the second alternative would require him to give up the notion of pure practical reason as being transcendent in the sense in which his theory requires.

How does this relate to the issue of the unqualified value of the good will? If the good will is unqualifiedly good, nothing can be added to it to make it better. This is the completeness criterion as a feature of the requirement that whatever is unqualifiedly good is the most fundamental good. Nothing can be the most fundamental good if something can be added to it to make it better. Yet on the current account of human dignity, something could be added to the good will to make it better, namely, the kind of qualities that render it vulnerable to integral stress. This cannot be done, however, without affording a kind of value to pathological features of our agency that Kantians cannot allow.

One might object that Kant makes a distinction between the highest good and unqualified value and that the distinction allows him to avoid the problem. The highest good, according to Kant, is a combination of a good will and happiness.[12] To put Kant's point in Aristotelian terms:

the best life is one of a good person living happily. According to this objection, something has gone wrong with my interpretation of Kant's conception of the most fundamental good because the most fundamental good would not seem to involve a completeness criterion: since a good will can be unqualifiedly good, and therefore the most fundamental good, without being the highest good, completeness is not entailed by fundamentality.

The problem with this objection is that the point about the highest good and the most fundamental good is not sufficient to undermine the relationship I claim exists between the most fundamental good and the completeness criterion. True, there is a completeness criterion that applies to the concept of the highest good that does not apply to the concept of the most fundamental good in Kant's sense. That one can be perfectly good on his view without being perfectly happy shows this. Nevertheless, this does not show that there is not another completeness criterion regarding unqualified goodness. Here it cannot be true that something could be the most fundamental good and yet derive any of its value from having something added to it that would make it better. On Kant's view, happiness is not a feature of the will such that a good person's finding happiness is a case of a will having something added to it, let alone making it better. The will is the same, happy or unhappy. Whatever is better by the addition of happiness, it is not the will. It remains complete in its unqualified goodness. What I am arguing is that a reasonably understood conception of dignity would add something to the good will as interpreted by Kant that would make it better, namely, qualities that bring with them vulnerability that is not possible with the concept of pure practical reason. The good will, properly understood, is vulnerable in ways that the Kantian scheme cannot accommodate. Part of the plausibility of the opening of Kant's *Groundwork* derives from the fact that at that stage comments regarding the good will are not as theoretically specific regarding the nature of the good will as they later come to be. Early on we tend to assent to some general judgments regarding the good will vaguely understood. Later, we think we have already assented to the good will having features that come with Kant's theory. With careful reflection we do not have to see the general claims about the good will and its unqualified value being tied to the specific conception of the good will as interpreted by Kant. Even stronger, careful reflection will reveal that the good will as interpreted by Kant cannot have features of agency we value most as a part of our dignity.

CHAPTER 6

Dignity and the Pathology of Respect

I.

A shift in approach might illustrate better the point about the pathology of our dignity-conferring qualities. In the earlier chapters on personal love and integral breakdown, I tried to show that the pathology of personal love is something we admire in persons. That loving qualities are pathological does not mean that loving people are wantons in Harry Frankfurt's sense[1] or sentimental idiots incapable of strength of character: one simply cannot be a loving person without great strength. It does mean, however, that the quality of being a loving person involves a limitation threshold regarding integral breakdown: if a person did not break down under some conceivable conditions, it would signify the absence of both love and a good quality of character. I tried to illustrate my point in this regard in several ways, but primarily with the character Sophie from William Styron's novel *Sophie's Choice*. I would like now to do something similar regarding the concept of respect. I would like to focus on what we admire in people in the way of dignity when we respect them and how our openness to the value of others in this regard renders us vulnerable to integral stress. If we admire people and afford them dignity, at least in part, because of their capacities for respecting others, and if respecting others and their dignity involves vulnerability to benign integral breakdown, then we admire people and afford them dignity for their vulnerability. I will focus discussion on phenomena surrounding grief and sorrow, on the one hand, and shame and contempt, on the other.

That grief is a response to integral stress no one should doubt. That it can be managed, that it can be endured, that the emotional disruption it brings to life can most often, with enough good fortune, be eventually overcome by people of good character should likewise be beyond doubt. These facts, however, should not blind us to the value we place on the human capacities that render people of good character vulnerable to the devastating effects of grief. If we are careful to distinguish grief from self-pity and other self-indulgent emotions, few of us would find a person incapable of the effects of grief anything other than some sort of emotional monstrosity. That admirable people are vulnerable to grief is part of what we respect in them; it is a constitutive element of their dignity-conferring qualities. In respecting these qualities, we are respecting pathological features of human character. What I take this to show is that our dignity-conferring qualities—qualities that are the objects of our sense of respect—are not confined to our rational capacities.

This is not to deny that our rational capacities are dignity conferring and objects of respect. It is, however, to assert that there is a limit to the role that rationality, as understood along Kantian or any other lines, plays in our judgments of respect in this regard. A person who lacked any rational capacity to manage grief under plausibly favorable circumstances would probably be met more with pity than with respect. Indeed, it is hard to see how a person who has no capacities for coping with difficulties of this sort, no matter how favorable the conditions of life might otherwise be, could be met with respect. This much speaks in favor of the Kantian line. Yet if we pay attention to the implausibility of lapsing into the other extreme, the Kantian view is difficult to defend.

The extreme to which I refer is the one according to which rationality is understood as a kind of control that transcends both in power and in value the value we place on our sentiments. Here I mean a conception of rationality that regulates our emotions and attachments to others in a way that makes us invulnerable to integral stress. In this regard, the Kantian view is much like what seems, at least at first glance, to be the Stoic view: pathological attachments to others that render us vulnerable to integral stress are inconsistent with a rational view of things and are thereby impediments to living the best or the right kind of life.

Seneca, especially, had a very dim view of the capacity for grief as a trait of character. In Epistle LXIII, "On Grief for Lost Friends," he said, "You have buried one whom you loved; look about for someone to love. It is better to replace your friend than to weep for him." A little later he confesses, "He who writes these words to you is no other than I, who wept so excessively for my dear friend Annaeus Serenus that in spite of my wishes, I must be included among the examples of men who have been overcome by grief. To-day, however, I condemn this act of mine and I understand that the reason why I lamented so greatly was chiefly that I had never imagined it possible for his death to precede mine."[2] Unlike Kant, Seneca's view of the irrationality of grief was that it is incompatible with an untroubled life.

The Kantian problem with grief or any pathological feature of our psychology is that it threatens our rational capacities for being agents of pure practical reason. The Kantian view, then, is that pathological influences on our character must always be under the control of reason as he understands it for us to view them as morally tolerable.

My claim, however, is that our attitude toward the capacity for grief is nothing like this. It is not so much that we think that some level of grief is not impermissible and therefore tolerable. What we think is that persons who love others in ways that render them vulnerable to devastating grief are the way they are in terms of something good about them, something that is central to their dignity, something that is worthy of respect. We do not view Sophie's grief as self-indulgent, self-serving, or romantic reveling. Also, we view with suspicion a person who is not so vulnerable. Furthermore, while it might be true that we admire people for elements of their character that have nothing to do with such vulnerability, I do not believe we ever respect anyone *in virtue of such invulnerability* or find any source of dignity in it.

So it is one thing to respect others because they have some degree of control over their emotions and thus to respect them for their rationality. Just as it is one thing to withhold respect for those who lack any such degree of rational control and to see them as lacking dignity. Yet neither of these points establishes the Kantian position regarding the nature of practical reason. To establish the Kantian position, one must afford a level of control over emotions that is inconsistent with the value we place on the qualities of character of which grief in particular is a function. That a loving parent should train her sentiments to cope with the fact that her children will someday die, that they will meet with significant setbacks, even that they might suffer from a certain amount of unpredictable bad luck is one thing. That they might meet with the most unexpected bad luck and horrifying dangers is quite another. To train one's sentiments in a way that if the latter occurs one can stand by one's normal obligations is to take a course toward eliminating those sentiments.

Moreover, it is both to exaggerate the role that our rational capacities play in terms of the value of dignity and to grossly overlook the role our pathological features play in that regard. What the Kantian must say is that we cannot rationally afford intrinsic value of the sort I claim we do to these pathological features of our character. Yet we do; these features are part of what we value most about persons in terms of their dignity even after reflection. Thus neither the idea of a transcendent God nor the idea of transcendent rationality models very well our concept of human dignity.

Very important, this point applies no matter what the metaphysics behind the concept of transcendent rationality. Many contemporary Kantians want to preserve transcendent rationality without the Kantian metaphysics.[3] They find Kantian metaphysics embarrassing to the defense of Kantian moral theory, so they do not want to talk about noumenal selves. Thus they think that the front line of defense is to separate the moral theory from the metaphysics. Yet even assuming that this could be done, it would provide no defense against the current objection to the concept of pure practical reason. Why? Because my objection does not go through the metaphysics to the moral theory; it goes straight to the moral theory itself: we do not place the value on transcendent rationality—the ability to manage the pathology of our sentiments—to the degree that Kantians claim we do when it comes to judgments of human dignity, and we do place a value on nontranscendence that Kantians claim we do not in such judgments.

The comments on grief show this in one way. Vulnerability to grief is a function of having loving qualities, and we admire people for being so vulnerable. The Kantian view is that we admire people for coping with the vulnerability well, not for the vulnerability itself. But connectedness in the form of personal love is something that is not just fodder for our dignity-conferring qualities; it is dignity conferring in its own right. Earlier discussion has shown this. So, in a way, both Hume and Kant were wrong: reason has more than the instrumental value of serving the passions, as Hume would have it, but it is not the sole bearer of our dignity, as Kant would have it. What I want to do now is to see if this point about grief as a kind of sorrow can be extended to a form of sorrow closer to the concept of respect. My question is this: is there a form of sorrow that is a function of respect in the way that grief is a form of sorrow that is a function of love? That is, are respectful agents vulnerable to integral stress through sorrow and their respectful capacities in a way similar to that in which loving persons are vulnerable to integral stress through grief and their loving capacities? If the answer is yes, where the respect attaches to human dignity, then it will be more plausible to think of respect as having a pathology of its own not captured on the Kantian model. If this is true, then the value we place on the human capacity for respecting self and others as a dignity-conferring quality is not best accounted for on a model of transcendent rationality.

II.

That there is a relationship between our concept of love and the capacity for the sorrow involved in grief is clear enough; but that there is a similar relationship between our concept of respect and sorrow is not. One very complicating factor is the concept of sympathy and the vulnerabilities to which it renders an agent having it among his or her sentiments and affective capacities.

It should be uncontroversial that generalized sympathy as a component in one's psychology has a pathology that renders one vulnerable in ways that are not completely under one's control. It should also be uncontroversial that some level of pathological sympathy is part of what we admire in people. Finally, it should be clear that generalized sympathy is not as central to our pathology as personal love, even among those we admire most. We would be puzzled by those who could sympathize with complete strangers but who were impervious to the weal and woe of those they allegedly love. Moreover, we would be puzzled not just about what kind of psychological creatures they were but over what value to place on their character should they simply be incapable of personal love but rather sensitive to generalized benevolence. Nonetheless, our conception of a fully admirable person includes a significant place for generalized sympathy. This means that our conception of a fully admirable person includes a significant place for the vulnerabilities to which the pathology of sympathy exposes one.

What does this have to do with respect and the pathology I allege it to have? Observations about sympathy are relevant here if it can be shown that within the psychology of those we admire most there is a symmetrical regulating influence between generalized sympathy and impartial respect. This would show that the pathology of sympathy is shaped by the psychological influence of respect, but it would also show that the capacity for respect is shaped by the pathology of sympathy. More centrally: if the capacity for respect among those we admire most is shaped in part by the pathology of generalized sympathy, then respect itself is a pathological feature of our psychology.

As to the regulating influence of impartial respect and our capacities for sympathy, our ability to sympathize with others is regulated to a significant degree by our ability to respect others. Those we find contemptible, we find it difficult to sympathize with. This is a factual claim about the relationship between two psychological capacities. Utter contempt eclipses the capacity for sympathy, rendering it difficult to impossible for a respectful person to sympathize with the Satanic character once there is a clear picture of what such a character is like. To this degree the pathology of sympathy is regulated by the capacity for respect in persons in whom both the capacity for generalized sympathy and the capacity for impartial respect are psychologically instantiated.

Of course, it might be possible that someone lacks the capacity for viewing others from the perspective of respect but is very attuned to others in a way that evokes sympathy. If so, surely the Kantians are right that such sympathy and the kind of pathology it displays are not to be found among the most admirable of persons. To be attuned to the pain of others with an eye to relieving it but without any regard to issues of merit is a vice, not a virtue. Teachers who inflate grades in a way that equally rewards excellence and mediocrity because they cannot cope with the disappointment of those who do not score well on reasonable criteria are neither respectful nor do they have sympathy instantiated in their psychology in a way that we admire. Such sympathy is not a virtue simply because it is not properly regulated by respect, and, most important, there is little about the pathology of such a person that we admire.

Nor can I see much that is admirable about sympathizing with the pain of clearly corrupt individuals when the corruption has reached a certain level and the pain is commensurate with the corruption. The tendency to feel pity for the Hitlers, the Charles Mansons, the Jeffrey Dahmers of the world is predicated either on a mistaken understanding of just what these people are or were like or on sympathy unregulated by respect for those terrorized by these monsters. If it is the latter, it is a function of a deplorable pathology.

What these observations show, I believe, is not, as the Kantians would have it, that our respect for persons is for nonpathological features of their psychology. What follows is that we do not admire some pathological instantiations of sympathy within a psychology. This is compatible with the possibility that we admire other pathologies that might go with other psychological instantiations of sympathy. That we do admire such instantiations and their pathologies is revealed in the fact that our conception of respect itself reflects the regulating influence of sympathy within the psychologies of those we admire most.

Consider in this regard alternative conceptions of respect with varying degrees to which they reflect a regulating influence of generalized sympathy. On the one hand is a conception of respect that is totally unregulated by sympathy. A clear example would be a concept of respect for others that is merely concerned with noninterference with their autonomy. Some, but not all, versions of political libertarianism might be construed in this way. On this view, respect only motivates noninterference; it does not motivate assistance in the way of positive duties. Thus one could be a perfectly respectful person on this view without being at all sympathetic, and the door is left open to a conception of respect that is unregulated by the pathological influence of sympathy.

I doubt that there are even many political libertarians who would endorse this conception of respect as a feature of morality. Political libertarians need not endorse the calloused view that as personal moral agents we have only duties of noninterference and no duties of positive assistance. It is one thing to assert that it would be a moral failure to refuse to render aid where one can without great cost to oneself and another to assert that the state is justified in coercing people to render aid in such circumstances. My point is not that the libertarians are right about the enforcement of such obligations. Rather, my point is that even libertarians need not and, I suspect, do not endorse the kind of calloused view of respect that does not generate positive duties to others.

What seems to be missing from a conception of morality that leaves out positive duties is sufficient concern for others. There is not enough caring, it seems. Indeed, it seems that there is not enough sympathy for the plight of others, and if we had proper respect for others we would have more sympathy for them than is found in a conception of respect unregulated by sympathy for others.

Kant, of course, believes that we have positive duties toward others, but this creates a dilemma of which he seems relatively unaware. The tension is this: how can we have positive duties toward others without granting sympathy a regulating influence within our conception of respect? It seems that we must either deny that we have positive duties toward others or endorse a conception of practical reason according to which the demands of respect are influenced by the pathological features of sympathy. To assert the latter is to assert that we cannot truly respect others unless we are somewhat sympathetic in regard to them. Yet how can practical reason be "pure," that is, a function of our cognitive rather than our affective and conative capacities, and involve a regulated conception of respect for others? This would be to assert that practical reason in the form of respect for others is a function, at least in part, of our pathological affective capacities.

In the *Groundwork*, Kant is very much concerned to assert that the categorical imperative generates positive as well as negative duties toward others. He asks us to consider whether we could universalize a volition that would exclude positive duties. He says,

> Yet a fourth is himself flourishing, but he sees others who have to struggle with great hardships (and whom he could easily help); and he thinks "What does it matter to me? Let every one be as happy as Heaven wills or as he can make himself; I won't deprive him of anything; I won't even envy him; only I have no wish to contribute anything to his well-being or to his support in distress!" Now admittedly if such an attitude were a universal law of nature, mankind could get on perfectly well—better no doubt than if everybody prates about sympathy and goodwill, and even takes pains, on occasion, to practice them, but on the other hand cheats where he can, traffics in human rights, or violates them in other ways. But although it is possible that a universal law of nature could subsist in harmony with this maxim, yet it is impossible to *will* that such a principle should hold everywhere as a law of nature. For a will which decided in this way would be in conflict with itself, since many a situation might arise in which the man needed love and sympathy from others, and in which, by such a law of nature sprung from his own will, he would rob himself of all hope of the help he wants for himself.[4]

Interpreting the so-called volitional test that Kant employs here is notoriously difficult. It is clear that he wants the result to be that we have positive duties to render aid, that the test is more than mere conceivability of a maxim as a natural law in a system of nature that could sustain itself, and that the test is supposed to be a function both of our respect for others and of pure practical reason. Beyond this, however, clarity regarding the deliberative mechanisms of the procedure is hard to find.

What does seem clear to me is that the issue of whether the maxim in this case is universalizable on the volitional test turns on what conception of respect is embedded in the psychology of the agent running the test. If the agent has a conception of respect that is unregulated by sympathy, then should he find himself in dire circumstances needing the assistance of others, he simply will not see them as having an obligation to assist him or as being disrespectful toward him. Nor will he see himself as being obligated to render aid to others in such circumstances on pain of being disrespectful should he refuse assistance. The test and its rationality turn on how we describe the psychology of the agent running the test. To get the result Kant wants the agent must be described as having a conception of respect for others that reflects sympathy for them, where this sympathy makes it practically rational for the agent to render aid as an expression at once of both sympathy and respect. Thus sympathy must be more than an external "incentive" for doing the right thing or an epistemic means of discovering one's duty but a source of the normative dimensions of respect itself. Of course, whether one has such sympathy is contingent on the pathological features of the agent's psychology, and a fortiori so is the agent's respect.[5]

Now suppose that everyone had a conception of respect regulated in this way by sympathy for others. It would then be true that no one could universalize the maxim in question. Yet it would not follow from this that our belief that we have positive duties toward others is a function of pure practical reason. It would be a function of pathological features of our psychology. That this is reflected in our actual conceptual scheme seems evident to me in the fact that we are puzzled by those who could even entertain living a life of indifference to the woe of others and think such a life consistent with respect.

Kantians might respond here that I have misread the procedure. Properly understood, the procedure requires that I take into account the fact that there are contingent features involved in the agency of imperfectly rational beings, as we humans are. That we experience pain, that we can have our hopes dashed, that we can find ourselves in dire straits—all are among these contingencies. Moreover, that these contingencies obtain is available to us through our cognitive faculties with proper input from our ability to sympathize with others. Sympathy, then, plays the role of providing us with the appropriate input for what life might be like for some imperfectly rational beings. It does not follow from this, however, that sympathy plays a regulating role in our conception of respect; it merely plays an epistemic role, allowing us to have the appropriate understanding of the variables necessary for the decisions of pure practical reason.[6] Having this epistemic function in practical reason does not entail that sympathy is instantiated in our psychology in a way that renders us pathologically vulnerable.

It is questionable that sympathy could even play this epistemic role for us without rendering us vulnerable to integral breakdown. Yet this is not the point I want to pursue here. Nor do I want to argue that this response is not adequate to Kant. I think it is, or, at least, something quite like it is. What I want to argue is that it does not reflect our conception of respect.

If sympathy is confined to an epistemic role in moral reasoning, then, of course, it plays no motivational role. Also, if respect is confined in its intentional objects to rational beings, then sympathy plays no direct role in moral epistemology regarding nonrational beings. However, sympathy does play a direct role in moral epistemology regarding nonrational beings. Sympathy not only functions to inform us of what life is like for lower animals; it motivates us in regard to our behavior toward them simply because we do sympathize with them, at least the people we admire do. Kant is right, I believe, that respect is a valuational attitude fitting only to agents. For this reason, it is not respect that is the source of our concern for lower animals. Rather, it is sympathy. Also, for many of us, it is clear on reflection that sympathy for lower animals is sometimes more important, all things considered, than the autonomy of rational beings in the pursuit of their interests. If I neglect my pets in a way that causes them extreme pain, I have not interfered with their rational autonomy. Nonetheless, I have surely wronged them, especially if the price of their pain is merely the frustration of minor interests I might have; and I have wronged them, not by failing to have respect for their rational autonomy, but by being unsympathetic to their pain. Moreover, if my not neglecting my pets comes only at a cost to myself, then the requirement that I not neglect them is a restriction on my autonomy. Yet on what conception of respect would it be a lack of respect for rational beings to require of them that in the pursuit of at least their minor interests they not cause extreme pain to nonrational, lower animals? This illustrates clearly to my mind that our conception of respect is regulated by sympathy within the psychologies of those we admire most.

Of course, Kantians can say here that we have indirect duties not to neglect our pets or to cause undue suffering to lower animals. Such a strategy avoids giving sympathy for lower animals anything other than an epistemic role in our moral deliberations. On this view, we have no direct moral concern for lower animals; any moral concern we have for them is an indirect function of our concern for rational beings. Thus our knowledge of our duties to rational beings requires that we know what life might be like for lower animals in certain regards. Yet we do not need to care about lower animals in any intrinsic way; we need only sympathize with them in the minimal sense necessary to gain the appropriate information about how to treat them, given that how we treat them bears on how we treat rational beings.

My response is that I simply and flatly deny that this is true of our conception of respect. When people are cruel to animals, it is the animals that we take to be the victims, even if they are not rational beings. They are the objects of our concern. Our sympathy for them is direct, and we do not take such direct sympathy to be contrary to respect for persons even when this sympathy sometimes justifies restricting the autonomy of rational beings. What we have in such cases is a conception of respect that exhibits the regulative influence of sympathy.

If it is true, then, that our respect for persons is regulated by our sympathy for animals, then what reason is there for insisting that sympathy plays only an epistemic role in our moral deliberations regarding human beings? The only reasons I can see involve the concern to deny that our conception of respect recognizes that respectfulness as a good-making quality renders us pathologically vulnerable as a mode of caring about ourselves and others. To recognize this, however, is to recognize that our conception of respect is not founded in anything like pure practical reason.

III.

So far I have argued that our conceptions of sympathy and respect exhibit symmetrical regulative functions. That sympathy is respect regulated is reflected in two facts: our ability to sympathize with others is functionally related to our ability to respect others, and we think that sympathy unregulated by respect can lead us to do the wrong thing. That respect is sympathy regulated is also reflected in two facts: our sympathy for lower animals sometimes makes it rational for us to restrict the autonomy of rational beings, and our belief that we have positive duties of benevolence is best accounted for as an expression at once of both our sympathy and our respect. But how is all this related to integral breakdown? The answer is that, so understood, respect opens the door to sorrow in just the way that sympathy does. It also opens the door to guilt and shame for not being sufficiently sympathetic to those we respect.

If this is true, we can delineate at least four pathological features of our conception of respect: (1) our ability to sympathize with others is functionally related to our ability to respect others; (2) our ability to relate to others is functionally related to our ability to respect others; (3) our ability to relate to others is functionally related to our ability to respect ourselves; and (4) our ability to relate to our loved ones is

functionally related to our ability to respect them as respectful, sympathetic people.

Consider in this regard our attitude toward how sensitive persons
should be regarding whether they or others are respectful, sympathetic
people. Do we expect sensitivity to this to reflect a pathology with an
integral threshold that affects a person's ability to relate to himself or
herself and others? The answer, I believe, is overwhelmingly affirmative.

As I intend the question here, it applies only to points (2) through (4).
It does not apply to (1), because I want to focus on relationships more
substantial than those predicated merely on sympathy. I might sympathize with lower animals but be utterly incapable of having any substantial relationship with them. Even so, relationships based solely on
respectful sympathy can render one vulnerable to debilitating sorrow for
the plight of those severely unfortunate. Of course, it should be clear that
the inability to sympathize at all with others because one finds them
utterly contemptible and unworthy of even minimal respect gives little
hope for any more substantial relationship with them. But this is just the
point. Lack of respect for others cuts off the possibility of social relationships with them, and to the degree that one is isolated from others
through lack of respect for them, one is alone. Such loneliness can be
devastating for humans. Moreover, some forms of loneliness seem to be
a direct function of not having anyone to relate to as a fellow respectful
person. Just imagine the effects on an admirable person's psychology of
being trapped in a society of only highly intelligent, in some sense interesting people, but who were utterly unworthy of respect as respectful,
sympathetic people. Even if one had protection against them regarding
one's physical safety, there would be no escaping the effects of loneliness.
That we are vulnerable to such loneliness is evidence that our capacities
for respect are deeply pathological. Moreover, there is no way to remove
this vulnerability without removing a source of what we admire most in
people in terms of their capacities for respect.

Now consider (3), that our ability to relate to others is functionally
related to our ability to respect ourselves. People who suffer from severe
guilt, shame, and lack of self-respect have enormous difficulties relating
to people they consider worthy of respect. This is the flip side of the fact
that our ability to relate to others is in part a function of our ability to
respect them. Just as we have an aversion to relationships with those we
do not respect, we expect others to have an aversion to those they do
not respect. Also, if we have respect for others but little or none for ourselves, we will think of others as rightfully having an aversion to rela-

tionships with us. The thought, then, that we are unworthy of relationships with others is a direct function of our lack of self-respect, and it is a function of this thought that those suffering from self-contempt are aversive to relationships with others. This is the pathology of failure in self-respect among persons sensitive to issues of respectability.

Of course, the pathology can be removed, but only by removing the sensitivity to issues of respectability. Anyone not subject to integral breakdown as a function of the belief that he or she is utterly contemptible is simply a person who is devoid of the sensibilities of respect. Also, anyone who can maintain normal relationships with others on an ongoing basis and yet believe that they lack qualities essential to minimal self-respect is self-deceived, which is itself a form of integral breakdown. What would it be to believe that one had done what Jeffrey Dahmer did and be able to look in the faces of respectable people in the full light of the facts? Looking in the mirror would be hard enough, but to contemplate relations with respectable people would, I believe, be utterly impossible for anyone sensitive to issues of respectability.

There might have been a generation of psychologists who would have advocated removing this kind of stress by removing the capacity for it. Yet it is difficult to see how we can be respectable people at all without having a psychology vulnerable in this pathological way to our failings. I can see no way to make sense of this pathology on the model of pure practical reason. If pure practical reason is the locus of our moral worth and if pure practical reason is a purely cognitive function of consciousness, then how do we make any sense of attributing the pathology to a merely cognitive function? Failings in cognitive functions exhibit themselves in factual errors, misperceptions, and errant calculations of various sorts. On the other hand, psychological failings that go deep into what we both are and value in ourselves exhibit themselves in the inability to maintain unity of the self across the full gamut of cognitive, conative, and affective capacities. It is this full gamut with its pathological features that is the locus of our dignity.

Finally, consider (4), that our ability to relate to our loved ones is functionally related to our ability to respect them as respectful, sympathetic people.

In his book, *Born Guilty*,[7] Peter Sichrovsky reports interviews with children of Nazi parents who have been exposed for collaboration in war crimes.[8] Among these children are those who admire their parents even in the light of such knowledge. Still more frequent are those who do not. Some of the children refuse to admit the facts, whereas others admit the facts, love their parents, but are ashamed of them. Finally, there are those who admit the facts and are completely alienated from their parents. The last two groups are of most interest here, but it is important to note some points about the first two groups.

Those children who admit the facts but who nonetheless admire their parents are those who significantly share the fascist views of their parents. Accordingly, they tend to see the loss of the war as a great tragedy and are alienated from those nonfascists who run the society now. They feel condemned to live in a world of people for whom they lack even minimal tolerance—people for whom they have utter contempt. They live in either the hope or despair for fascist revival. Their lack of respect for others to whom they are not specially related affects them deeply, for they see themselves and their parents as the unjustly persecuted.

Those of the second group who refuse to admit the facts show by their reluctance that they cannot endorse the conception of respect endorsed by the first group. By contrast, their conception of respect requires that those with the qualities of the Nazi collaborators are contemptible people. Their knowledge of the facts threatens their very integrity, which is exhibited in the integral stress that leads to self-deception. The source of this stress is the threat of alienation from their parents and society. But if avoiding such alienation requires self-deception regarding their parents' qualities, then to that degree their self-deception constitutes integral breakdown. That it is not difficult to understand such self-deception shows how important we think the goods of respect for and by others are in the lives of people.

Now to the last two groups. The first is that group of children of former Nazis who admit the facts regarding their parents, who love them, but are ashamed of them. Sichrovsky does not report what percentage of the children interviewed fall into this category, but it is an important fact. How could people without the qualities of fairness, kindness, and sympathy toward strangers have other qualities necessary to establish a loving relationship with their children? The interviews make clear that many of the former Nazis did not have personally loving qualities. In these cases, there simply never was a loving relationship between many Nazi parents and their children. The children of these parents uniformly describe their parents as contemptible people, as people without any qualities worthy of respect. Besides, they often attribute the alienation they feel with other people to a lack of qualities in themselves resulting from being the children of such parents, and they, the children themselves, describe their lives as lives of desperation.

Those who do love their parents and who hold them in contempt experience a different kind of tension in their lives. They cannot live with their parents, nor can they live without them. They can neither endorse their relationships with their parents nor repudiate their relationships. Put another way, they both endorse their relationships with their parents and repudiate their relationships. They repudiate their parents for their crimes and for lacking the respectable qualities that would have prevented their crimes. At the same time they endorse their parents, not only because they love them but also because their parents have other qualities that are worthy of respect, namely, those of loving parents. The problem is that the simultaneous cognitive awareness of their parents as former Nazis *and* as loving parents does not allow the children to settle their thoughts about their relationship to their parents. This kind of disruption is the direct result of the children being unable to respect *as persons* those they most love. Here the thought that their parents are loving parents and respectable as such is not enough to settle the issue of what *kind* of persons their parents are. Nor is it enough to settle their thoughts regarding their relationship to their parents. It is also important to note that knowledge of the contemptible qualities of the parents is not sufficient for unequivocal repudiation either. Where to go with their lives in relationship to their parents is a constantly unresolved issue with them. This is pervasive in a way that precludes the kind of closure necessary for the unity of self for integrity. This is to say that most often it is coping with their relationship with their parents that sets the parameters for psychological survival. When the issue of survival is set in terms of such irreconcilable bifurcation, the practical orientation of a person cannot be that of an agent of integrity. This is because, for persons of this sort, their categorical commitments are incommensurable values that conflict at the very core of life. Moreover, unless there is substantial unity in that which gives a person's life meaning, there cannot be any hope for integrity until the conflict is resolved. This is integral stress at its most intense level.

Finally, there is the group of children who admit the facts regarding their parents' participation in war crimes and are alienated from them. Some of these children were alienated from their parents long before they knew the relevant facts regarding the war. They simply never had a loving relationship with their parents because they never had loving parents. I have already commented on these children. Here the concern is with those children who had loving relationships with their parents before coming to know the relevant facts regarding the war and afterward became alienated from them. The problem is that when the children are alienated from their parents it is not clear to what extent the discovery of the war crimes played a causal role in the alienation. This is due to the reaction of most, if not all, of the children. Few with loving relationships before learning of the war crimes could bring themselves to repudiate fully their relationships to their parents after discovering these crimes. These children, then, are victims of their parents' crimes in this sense: they are condemned to living a life of shame for persons they love most. On the other hand, many of those children who are alienated from their parents are also victims of their parents' war crimes in a different sense: they labor to remove themselves from responsibility for their parents when nothing seems from their point of view to count as adequate. Central to their identity is that they be exonerated for something they never did. But, of course, one can never be exonerated for that, and it is the fact that they cannot respect their parents that sets this task at the center of their lives.[9]

Perhaps some children of former Nazis with loving relationships with their parents before discovering the facts regarding their crimes later became alienated from them without this kind of victimization. If so, the alienation they experience from their parents allows these children to proceed with their lives without centering the past in such a disruptive and destructive way. If there are such children, they are indeed fortunate (at least from the perspective of their future). The interviews do not reveal such children.

What do we learn from a study of all these children about respect, human dignity, and pure practical reason? First, we should recognize that the tragedy is not the same in all the cases. Those who admire their parents in full light of the facts are simply people of bad character, however tragic the explanation for that might be. Those who avoid the facts through self-deception are also people of bad character, although the need for self-deception might itself reflect an element of something good in them, namely, that they cannot live with the thought that their parents are contemptible people. Given other weaknesses in one's character, one's virtues might trigger self-deception. Still, this is malignant breakdown.

But what are we to say about the children who love their parents but cannot cope with what their parents have done? Are we to think of them as self-indulgent, self-serving, revelers in romanticism, as comments by Seneca and Kant might suggest?[10] Or are we to take their stress seriously? How is it possible to construe their psychological difficulties as anything other than a function of what is good about them? More specifically, how is it possible to construe these difficulties as anything other than a function of their capacities for respect? What vice could be removed that would eliminate the stress? Or what exceptional virtue could be added that would make them immune to effects that have clearly made them less strong than they could otherwise have been had fortune been more benevolent to them? In short, how could we change them without an assault on those qualities essential to their dignity?

It is utterly inexplicable how an improvement in the cognitive capacities of these children could relieve the stress, even if we thought psychological immunity to such stress desirable, which we do not. It is simply impossible to assign the dignity we do to human beings, to assign the capacities of being loving, sympathetic, respectful people, and to assign unqualified value only to the cognitive dimensions of our persons. We are not nearly as Platonic, Kantian, and Christian as the conception of pure practical reason insists, and we never have been. Despite the influence of otherworldly traditions, we have always valued, inconsistently to be sure, those aspects of persons that render us vulnerable to benign integral breakdown. Nowhere is the evidence more compelling than in the pathology of our capacities for respect.

IV.

When we bring these thoughts back to the issue of unqualified goodness, things are not nearly so clear as the opening of Kant's *Groundwork* would lead us to believe. I am not at all sure that we should accept the condition that human dignity is nothing unless it is based on unqualified goodness in Kant's sense. Nor am I sure that we have a clear and distinct idea about what the value of human dignity is. What we value in ourselves and others such that we think in terms of dignity is an extremely difficult problem for which there are now only partial answers. Accepting this fact is hard for all of us. We want it to be true that we have a perfectly clear idea of that which we value in ourselves and others as the basis for our dignity, even if we cannot prove that we have such value. The Kant in all of us might even want a conception of dignity that is clear enough to generate a rational decision procedure for morality for all occasions. Yet reflection reveals, I believe, that we must accept the fact that the value we place on humans as having dignity is an important but vague value.

Nor is it clear that the locus of the value we place on human dignity, vague or not, is the human will. This is especially so if the will is understood as a function of a unique kind of moral concern, whether that concern is spelled out in terms of pure practical reason or in terms of some other concern. Indeed, it seems from what has been said that if anything has unqualified value and if that thing is a will, then an unqualifiedly good will is the will of a person with a certain character. No will without character, and no good will without good character. Moreover, the character of a good person is one in which the regulative influences involving his or her willings are symmetrically related. Neither unregulated love, unregulated sympathy, nor unregulated respect is of unqualified value. If, and this is a rather big if, anything has unqualified value and that thing is a will, it is a will that is not only respectful but loving, sympathetic, and caring in other ways where these modes of caring reflect the influence of other concerns within the psychology of the agent. Such symmetry, however, carries with it a network of a rather hardwired pathology. An indeterminate pathology to be sure, one with wide parameters and significant malleability, but nonetheless one the boundaries of which are not extendable or retractable, even ideally, at the prompts of a purely cognitive capacity of our being. In this sense, a good will is good for its impurity rather than its purity. We are not gods but animals, and our dignity is in the kind of animals we are.

CHAPTER 7

The Possibilities of Therapy

Epicurean Strategies

At this point, one might think that I have overstated the case for vulnerability. What is needed, it might be argued, is therapy for those susceptible to integral breakdown of whatever variety. A properly understood clinical psychology, the objection continues, will reveal a treatment whereby no one need suffer from what I call benign integral breakdown. On this hypothesis, the availability of a successful clinical psychology that would eliminate the vulnerabilities without eliminating virtues would refute my claim that there is benign integral breakdown.

The purpose of the remainder of this book is to address this objection by considering recent attempts to revive some central elements of Hellenistic ethics. My strategy will be to evaluate two versions of "extirpation therapy" and to argue that there is no version of any such therapy that can succeed *both* at retaining traits that we intrinsically value most in persons and at avoiding attributing integral thresholds that render agents vulnerable to benign integral breakdown. Also, I will argue that the most promising therapeutic model for coping with stress is one that aims not at invulnerability as such but at minimizing integral stress consistent with retaining that which we value most in ourselves and others. Finally, I shift the burden to those who would advocate some other form of therapy to tell us what its therapeutic strategy is.

I.

The extirpation model is one advocated by pure forms of Stoicism and in part by Epicureanism, philosophical views currently enjoying a revival of interest and attention by some very serious moral philosophers. Here I am thinking primarily in terms of the recent work of Julia Annas in *The Morality of Happiness* and Martha Nussbaum in *The Therapy of Desire*. Although it would be difficult for me to overstate my high opinion of the contributions of these two books to contemporary moral philosophy, my primary goal here is to criticize the prospects for views thought to be promising by Annas and Nussbaum.

I begin, then, with the extirpation model in its Epicurean and Stoic forms, limiting myself in this chapter to Epicureanism and taking up Stoicism in the next. Some precautionary comments are in order, however. Classifying philosophical alternatives by appeal to historical thinkers and their works is risky business. Take utilitarianism, for example. Historically, the name most commonly associated with utilitarianism is John Stuart Mill, and the work most commonly associated with that philosophical school is Mill's *Utilitarianism*. Yet there is good reason for the debate over whether the balance of the view presented by Mill in that work is really utilitarian or Aristotelian, especially the second chapter on the theory of value. The issue is whether utilitarianism can accommodate an ordinal ranking of preferences or pleasures according to kind; the problem is remaining sufficiently neutral regarding individual well-being to avoid conflating the distinction between what is uniquely utilitarian and what is Aristotelian. That Alfred North Whitehead was a Whiteheadean there can be no doubt, just as there can be no doubt that Mill was a Millian. Nevertheless, there can be doubt about whether Mill was the best representative of utilitarianism.

A similar problem arises regarding Hellenistic ethics and its progeny, depending on whether we take as representatives of the various schools of thought Greek or Roman thinkers. In general, I believe that it is better to take the Greek thinkers as the best representatives of departures from Aristotle regarding the salient points of theoretical difference than the Roman. This is to say that if we want to know what hedonism as a philosophical alternative is in the debate among the ancients, we get a purer statement of its tenets from a judicious reading of views attributed by Cicero and others to Epicurus than from the writings of Lucretius. Yet it is not to say that we get a richer philosophical view in the former than in the latter; just as it is not to say that Jeremy Bentham's thought, though purer in utilitarian form, is richer philosophically than Mill's. Similarly, if we want to know what Stoicism is as a philosophical alternative to Aristotelianism in the debate among the ancients, we get a purer statement of its central tenets in an understanding of Chrysippus than in the writings of Seneca.

II.

These comments are especially important as they bear on the prospects for a therapeutic model. The Epicureans impugned emotional attachments that were generally of negative hedonic value on the grounds that they were predicated on false beliefs.[1] Without defending the claim to historical accuracy, I will construe the value of any emotion in a life well lived on an Epicurean view to be the hedonic value of instantiating that emotion within the psychology of a person in an ongoing life. Those emotions that would have a negative hedonic value on balance are to be extirpated. Epicurean therapy, then, aims at removing the false beliefs that lead to emotions of negative hedonic value. Religious beliefs that place a value on an afterlife were special targets of the Epicureans, but so were other beliefs that are embedded in the emotional structure of certain emotions. Pure Epicurean therapy, then, aims at removing any false beliefs that lead to the fear of death or any other emotion that has a generally negative hedonic value. This opens the inquiry into which emotional attachments feed the fear of death. I take the Epicurean model to aim at removing any emotional attachment that feeds fearful attitudes toward dying. Any model that departs from this requirement is not pure Epicureanism because it must either reject the view that the fear of death has a generally negative hedonic value or accept as relevant some non-hedonic value as more important to a life well lived than avoiding the fear of death.

Another tenet of Epicureanism that leads to extirpation is that well-being is not quantifiable in the sense that more of a good life is better. For one thing, they thought it false that the ending of a good life was a loss *to* someone: if so, to whom?[2] Moreover, they thought it a source of misery that we live in anxiety that our future will not be as good as our past. Therefore, the belief that more of a good life is better is a false belief that is generally of negative hedonic value and is to be extirpated along with the fear of death. The fear of death, then, and the desire to go on living, even where life's continuance would be more of a good thing, are irrational barriers to a life well lived that are to be extirpated on the

Epicurean model of therapeutic psychology. On Nussbaum's interpretation, Lucretius is appealing, I believe, only because he does not accept the full implications of Epicureanism in regard to both the fear of death and the desire to continue a life well lived.[3] Nonetheless, it is instructive to consider the values that psychologically feed the fear of death and the desire to continue a meaningful life.

The structure of the Epicurean therapeutic strategy centers on isolating those factors of consciousness that provide the best grips for the extirpation process. For the Epicureans, these are beliefs. By removing false beliefs, we are able, on their view, to remove those sources of dissatisfaction that impede the life of pleasure. We need not endorse their view that emotions *are* beliefs to take their strategy seriously. All we need is to take seriously that there is a cognitive dimension involving beliefs that are central to various emotions and attitudes and that removing these beliefs can dismantle the emotions.

The model looks something like the following. For any emotion, E, psychologically instantiated in some agent, A, there is some belief or set of beliefs, B, apart from which E cannot be sustained in A. Thus for any emotion, E, that has generally negative hedonic value and thus is an obstacle to A's living a life of flourishing, E can be extirpated by showing A that B is false. Thus philosophy is understood on a medical model, as Nussbaum's book is concerned to emphasize in regard to the Epicureans: the philosopher is the physician responsible for removing false beliefs that impede the hedonically good life.

As the model has been presented, however, there is some ambiguity regarding beliefs. The ambiguity involves how we are to understand beliefs. Are they merely descriptive or evaluative in content? Suppose, for example, that I fear someone because I believe that he has the intention of hurting me. Assuming that my belief is false, that is, that this person does not in fact have the intention of hurting me, the fear is most easily removed by showing me that my belief is false. Also, if I fear death because I have the religious belief that an afterlife of eternal torment awaits me, my fear of death can be removed by removing the religious belief, assuming that there is no other source for my anxieties regarding death.

However, we should contrast different cases of believing that _____ (where the blank is filled in with a grammatical proposition). Believing that *someone intends to hurt me* and believing that *pain is bad* is the kind of contrast I have in mind. It is a contrast between a factual belief and an evaluative belief; and the task of extracting beliefs of the first sort because they are false is not like the task of extracting beliefs of the second sort. The first is clearly an epistemological project, whereas the second is something at least somewhat different. To extract beliefs of the second sort, sometimes one has to extract values that are psychologically instantiated within the person. In fact, the instantiation of emotions within a psychology involves both well-placed beliefs and values. Fear of pain involves both believing that there are things that can hurt you and disvaluing pain. Similarly, fear of death involves factual beliefs regarding the consequences of death, but it also involves values placed on those things affected by death, among them, of course, is one's life. It is very important to realize about this that not all cases of removing the factual beliefs attendant on an emotion are rational. This is simply because sometimes these beliefs are true. It is not rational to extirpate my fear of someone by removing my belief that he intends to hurt me, if indeed he intends to hurt me. This is because the value of avoiding pain is, on some interpretation, one both we and the Epicureans want to retain. Thus, if one is a hedonist, the fear of pain is one that can only be moderated by the extirpation of false belief; it is not itself a candidate for extirpation.

III.

But what about the fear of death? One extirpation strategy might be simply to take factual beliefs that feed the fear of death one at a time and show that they are all false. I doubt very seriously that this will succeed in itself, for it assumes that there are no evaluative beliefs that, when combined with true factual beliefs, feed the fear of death. The idea here is to have a strategy that is confined to removing nonevaluative beliefs. On this view, the therapist does not have some general set of factual beliefs in mind as beliefs to be extirpated. Instead, the therapist must discover in each individual case what factual beliefs feed the fear of death and show that they are false.

An alternative strategy is to take as one's task showing that death itself is either a good thing or at least not a bad thing. This would be to admit that the fear of death cannot be rationally extirpated, even ideally, by eliminating all false factual beliefs from a person's belief repertoire. It would also be to recognize that part of the task of extirpation, if the fear of death is to be removed as a significant source of pain and negative hedonic value, is the removal of some of the values psychologically embedded in emotions. That this would be part of the task of any plausible Epicurean hedonism seems undeniable, especially regarding the fear of death as it arises from religious beliefs. If we fear death not because we fear eternal torment but because we believe that death would terminate our relationship with God and we value that relationship, what false factual belief once removed will remove the fear? The belief that we have such a relationship might be false, but removing it would seem only to exacerbate things hedonically for the religious believer. If religious belief plays a role here in the fear of death, it would seem that it is not the factual belief that we have a relationship with God, but the value belief that a never-ending relationship with God is a good thing. To remove this kind of belief, however, involves removing values that are psychologically embedded in the emotions of the religious believer. Just what those emotions and values are and what the strategy is for performing this task is not entirely clear.

We might try to show that after reflection there is *no* plausible coherent set of values that would make eternal life a good thing for human beings. Thus showing the incoherence of a value belief would be a way to remove it and constitute another way in which an emotion can be extirpated than by removing false factual beliefs. Any successful argument of this sort regarding the fear of death would yield the result that, for any human life, death at some point is a good thing.[4] Let us assume that any reflective analysis of our values, even those embedded in emotions that survive the call for extirpation, will in fact yield this result and that death at some point is a good thing. The most such an analysis could achieve is the extirpation of the desire to live forever. That this is progress, I do not deny, and if successful, it represents a devastating assault on many religious views. Also, it illustrates well that extirpation of values by means of philosophical reflection on them can be sage advice and efficacious therapy regarding our desires. Yet it is one thing to assert that extirpation of some desires is a proper goal of philosophical therapy and quite another to assert that the removal of an emotion like the fear of death from our entire repertoire of emotions is.

IV.

As Nussbaum recognizes, left in place after the extirpation of the desire to live forever are the desire to live longer and the fear of dying too soon. One might think that the kinds of values that when coupled with true beliefs feed the desire to live longer and thereby the fear of dying too soon are like the values that generate the desire to live forever. If this is true, then the proper candidate for extirpation is not simply the fear of not living forever but the fear of death itself. But it is completely implausible that the values in each case are analogous, which means that the task of extirpation must be different for the fear of not living forever and the fear of dying too soon.

Consider how the values are different. In the case of the desire to live forever, the values must be such that they could sustain the desire to live throughout eternity. The argument against this is that on any values that are accessible to us, it is difficult to see how they could be sustained without the anticipation of death. My point here is not to endorse this argument, though I believe that reflection will reveal that it is a good one. Rather my point is that it is implausible that such an argument could serve to undermine the desire to live longer and the fear of dying too soon. Why? Because there are many clear values that death would come as a blow to if death came too soon *and* that it would not come as a blow to if things went on forever. Moreover, these same values make it rational for us to desire to continue a life well lived, which is contrary to the other Epicurean tenet: that more of a good life is not better.

Suppose I take both pride and delight in completing an intellectual project, say, finishing this manuscript. Death can come too soon by coming before I finish. We can admit this without committing ourselves to the view that writing philosophy is a value that could make life meaningful throughout eternity. Philosophy is rich, but not that rich. This is one way, then, that a value embedded in an emotion can generate the desire to live longer and the fear of dying too soon without generating the desire to live forever. The love we have for our children, our parents, and our friends is similar. My love for my daughter includes my valuing her future welfare, and part of that welfare involves my continued existence: to be there when she needs me, to share her achievements, to reciprocate her affections, especially during her childhood and youth. Death can come too soon by preventing me from filling this place in her life. Similarly, my death can affect the welfare of my parents by taking away from them something central to the meaning of their lives. Loving them involves my valuing the fact that this does not happen to them, which provides a basis for my desire to live longer and for my fear of dying too soon. Yet, here again, we can admit this without believing that the value of parent/child relations is such that it could fill eternity with meaning. Such an analysis also extends to marital love and friendship. Barring special circumstances, my love for my wife involves my valuing a relationship with her that extends over some significant and indefinite period of time. Yet neither she nor I need think that our love would survive eternity. All we need for a desire to go on living is that a love exists between us now that projects itself into the foreseeable future. It is one thing for an emotion to project its values indefinitely into the future and quite another for it to project them into eternity. All the emotions referred to here involve values that can generate the desire to go on living and the fear of dying too soon, without involving factual beliefs that are false. Extirpating these emotions, then, cannot be achieved by removing false factual beliefs and incoherent values.

It might be objected, however, that I have overlooked an alternative according to which the distinction between factual beliefs and value beliefs as I have been using it is a bogus distinction. To be sure, there are value beliefs that are distinct from some factual beliefs that are embedded in our emotions and desires. But it does not follow from this, so the objection goes, that the value beliefs that are embedded in our emotions are not just special kinds of factual beliefs to be distinguished only from some other kinds of factual beliefs. "That is a hammer" and "that is a bad hammer" have all the marks of being distinguished as a factual belief versus an evaluative belief. When we realize, however, that the latter attributes only instrumental value, we realize that it too is a factual belief, whatever else it is: it is, after all, true or false that any particular hammer can serve the hammering function well. Of course, whether we care about the fact of whether any particular hammer serves the hammering function well turns on our valuing some conception of a hammering function. But given such valuing, the belief that the hammer is good is both factual and evaluative.

How are we to understand the concept of instrumental value here and its role in extirpation therapy? If we are hedonists, we have a view of the proper function of emotions and desires: their function is to provide a psychological framework in which life can be lived in the best way possible on hedonic criteria. Thus emotions and any values embedded in them are ultimately of only instrumental value. To be sure, if we confine ourselves to the perspective of any particular emotion, the values embedded in them are intrinsic values: loving one's children means intrinsically valuing their future welfare, and so on. Yet we might view any positive emotion as including the value belief that that emotion itself is essential to a life well lived. This would mean that there are at least two kinds of value beliefs internal to any positive emotion: (i) a belief that the object internal to the emotion is intrinsically good, and (ii) a belief that the intrinsic valuing of the objects internal to emotions is conducive to a life well lived. If we specify some theory of value for judgments about a life well lived, both kinds of value beliefs are straightforwardly true or false; and this is just what the hedonist does.

Thus if parental love intrinsically values a child's future welfare, but a life in which that emotion is psychologically instantiated is not in fact of generally positive hedonic value, then the intrinsic value judgment of parental love is false. A large part of the Epicurean argument for this would be that since emotions of this sort do feed the fear of death, the pain they carry with them in that regard undermines their positive hedonic value. Extirpation aims at removing this false factual/evaluative belief regarding the hedonic benefits of intrinsically valuing one's beloved children. By so doing it aims at extirpating both the positive emotion of parental love and the negative emotion of the fear of dying too soon, the latter being a function of the former.

V.

There are at least two lines of attack, either separately or in conjunction, that can be employed in response to this. The first is to deny that an adequate analysis of emotions yields the result that there are value beliefs of the second sort embedded in them as part of their structure. That is, an adequate analysis of emotions will not yield the result that internal to any positive emotion is an evaluative belief to the effect that attachments of the sort expressed in the emotion itself are intrinsic to a life well lived. The second response is to admit that there are such value beliefs internal to the emotions themselves but to deny that what makes a life well lived is its hedonic qualities.

The criterion by which the first issue is to be settled is anything but immediately clear. What would show that the claim that positive emotions contain an affirmation of their status within a life well lived is false? Or, alternatively, what would show that the denial of this claim about emotions is false?

Perhaps some insight into answers to these questions can be gained by asking analogous questions about the first sort of value beliefs associated with emotions. What confirms that if P has parental love for Q, then, under normal circumstances, P cares about Q's future welfare in such a way that Q's future welfare is an intrinsic value to P? The answer must be that unless we are willing to attribute the value belief in question to P we are not willing to attribute the emotion of parental love to P. But what would count as showing that P has the value belief? Self-report will not do, because it is entirely possible that one's belief that one values another's future welfare could be true without it being true that one values another's future welfare. Unless we tell some very special story about mitigating circumstances, I cannot see what would count as evidence that P has such a value that would not include some behavioral evidence of anxieties on the part of P about either P's dying too soon or Q's dying too soon or both. Even if I have a child who I know is going to die too soon and even if I have come to grips with this fact in a way that allows me to appreciate the present without hope for the future, this does not show that I do not have the value in question. That is, this would not show that I am neither a loving parent nor one who does not value his child's future welfare. All it would show is that I have come to grips with my anxieties as generated by my love for my child. Moreover, complete indifference to prospects of the premature death of either my child or myself before I can play a significant role in my child's future welfare would be convincing evidence, barring some very special circumstances, that I did not love my child. The point is that there are behavioral tests for the presence of value beliefs of the first sort, and these tests are revealed in our willingness to attribute certain emotions to people.

I assume then that some such test is applicable to value beliefs of the second sort, that emotions themselves include value beliefs confirming or denying their place in a life well lived. Yet how are we to understand the test here in such a way that the thesis is falsifiable? A plausible conception of the evidence might be that anyone experiencing an emotion who continues to pursue a way of life that includes the values of the first sort relative to that emotion tacitly expresses an affirmation of the place of that emotion in a life well lived. On this view, if I continue to pursue a life that involves my caring deeply about my child's future welfare in a way that reflects that I love my child, I am thereby endorsing a way of life that includes emotional attachments of the parentally loving sort. It is the fact that parental love does give us reasons for action in this sense that reveals that the emotion itself includes its own self-endorsement in a life well lived. Emotions that do not provide us with such reasons for action do not carry with them their own self-endorsement.

Assuming that this is correct, what does it prove regarding the Epicurean conception of a life well lived and the extirpation of emotions, the fear of death in particular? There seems to be a dilemma. On the one hand, if my emotional endowment is such that I am not disposed to anxiety should there be a threat to my child's future welfare, then I do not love her. It is, after all, the fact that parental love generates anxiety related to the fear of death that presents such love as a candidate for extirpation. On the other hand, if I do love her, then my emotional endowment is such that it disposes me to anxiety for her future welfare should it be threatened in a way that gives me reasons for action. If the first is true, then there is no room for extirpating the fear of dying too soon by extirpating the parental love that generates that fear, for parental love is not present. If the second is true, then the judgment built into the emotion is that whatever values that prevent a life of parental love are not a part of a life well lived and hence the judgment gives the agent reasons for rejecting that alternative way of life. This includes an alternative way of life that excludes parental love but the fear of death as well. Thus it would seem that having an emotion, at least a very strong positive emotion, would be such that it would be instantiated within a psychology in a way that preempted certain forms of life from being deliberative alternatives from the perspective of the agent. If this is true, then there would be no room within the psychology of an agent in which such an emotion is instantiated for the question of extirpation to come up. Indeed, if the issue could come up, it would provide evidence that the emotion was not in place. All that would follow, then, from the second sort of value belief is that whatever else a life well lived includes it must include the values embedded in that emotion, which does not attribute instrumental value to emotional attachment in this regard at all. Rather it attributes a part/whole relationship between the intrinsic value of a life as a whole and the intrinsic value of a constituent part of that whole. Yet neither of these kinds of judgment is simply a variety of factual judgment.

It would seem that the kinds of emotions and desires that would generate the fear of dying too soon are just the kinds of emotions and desires that would preclude, from the perspective of an instantiated psychology, deliberations about the value of the objects of those emotions and desires. This is why they are categorical qualities of that particular psychology. Shatter them, and the psychology itself is shattered. Thus the incapacity to deliberate beyond a certain point is a function of the fact that some emotions and desires are categorical qualities of the psychology in which they are instantiated. This is why stress to these emotions and desires is integral stress.

Now consider parental love, the values internal to it, and the desires generated by those values. What would it mean to instantiate parental love, along with its values and desires, within a psychology but not as a categorical quality of that psychology? The Hellenistic philosophers are quite right, I think, to insist that where such love exists it exists as central to the psychological perspective in which it is embedded. Thinking of parental concern as somehow peripheral is perplexing unless one is thinking of people who are not loving parents. But if it is true that parental love is a categorical emotion of the psychology in which it is instantiated, it is also true that the values embedded in parental love are categorical values of that psychology. This means that these values place deliberative limits on the kinds of life that can be considered as deliberative alternatives for the person in whom these values are psychologically instantiated. If so, then the project of extirpating parental love cannot come up as a deliberative option for a loving parent. Moreover, this follows from the interpretation of the Epicurean analysis of emotions that we are considering.

VI.

Now it might be said that this argument overlooks the fact that the aversion to pain can also be categorically embedded within a psychology. Where it is, it might be argued, it can come into conflict with other categorical features that threaten to fracture that psychology. Seeing this about one's own psychology might lead one to take steps, painful as they might be in the short run, to alter one's psychology in a way that eliminates the pain by eliminating the emotion that feeds it.

The problem with this response is that even admitting the premise that the aversion to pain can be categorical within a psychology that includes parental love does not make it rational to extirpate the fear of death by extirpating parental love. Everything turns on what the degree of pain has to be to generate a categorical aversion to the way of life that includes it. Take two extremes. On the one extreme, imagine a person who cannot consider as a deliberative option a way of life that includes anything but minor aches and pains. Such a person is one in which the anticipation of anything but the most insignificant of pains causes integral stress of a sort that effectively preempts deliberation. If this is the psychology we are to imagine, then it is just false that this is a psychology in which parental love can be instantiated. People who are aversive of pain in this sense are simply incapable of parental love.

On the other extreme, imagine the person who is categorically aversive to pain only of the most horrifying sort. Such a person is one who can endure great pain if doing so is necessary in the service of his or her positive categorical values. Still, there comes a point at which even this kind of person cannot take the pain anymore. Threatened with a literal Hell, with a sampling of its punishment imaginatively projected into eternity, this person's positive values are eclipsed as deliberative variables and practical alternatives. Could a person who has this kind of categorical aversion to pain be a person within whose psychology personal love is instantiated? Only those completely unfamiliar with extreme pain could assert that loving parents have to be able to resist pain of this sort. Bernard Williams and Peter Unger have given us good reasons to think hard about the central role of pain in practical reason.[5] We would be naive to think that if pain were made intense and durable enough, other emotions, desires, and values could have the weight with us to yield the thought that it was to be endured.

Yet we can admit all this without accepting the Epicurean call to extirpate the fear of dying too soon that is due to emotions like parental love. For the fear of dying too soon is not normally a pain of the sort of the second extreme. Normally the anxieties of loving parents regarding either their or their children's dying too soon, while far from being insignificant aches and pains, are also far from being unbearable torture. Indeed, it is plausible that there are many pains that are far from unbearable torture that are part of a life that on balance includes more pain than pleasure. In fact, it seems the psychology in which an aversion to pain has this kind of on-balance sensitivity is one in which parental love cannot be instantiated. The deliberative limits of loving parents are such that the consideration of taking up a life that has this kind of on-balance credit in favor of pain avoidance at the cost of the essential well-being of his or her children is one that cannot, in any real sense, come up. If a person could deliberate about this, that is, actually give serious consideration to, say, taking a mind-altering drug that would prevent his or her ever caring about another in ways that generate the anxieties in question, this would be clear behavioral manifestation that parental love was absent. What a person *can* deliberate about can tell us as much about his or her psychology as what he or she cannot deliberate about.

Consider, in this regard, the anxieties of the following people. A and B are loving parents who are thinking about having another child. Both know what it has been like to worry about their first child's well-being, and both rightly believe that the prospects for an early death of a future child is statistically normal. They know also, however, that despite these prospects their next child could be the exception that drives down the average. If we hold all the other variables that might be involved in such a decision constant, do we expect the anxiety regarding the probabilities to render these parents rationally aversive to having another child? Suppose A, due to both a persistent desire for another child and lingering anxieties of this sort, decides to go for therapy to extirpate the source of these anxieties. It is difficult to see how to imagine this if we imagine A to be a loving parent. The reason it is difficult is that removing the source of her anxieties would radically undermine her relationship to her present child. The consideration of therapy might be greater as the probabilities of premature death increase when there is no present relationship. If someone were filled with the capacity for parental love but lived in an environment where the probabilities for premature death were virtually certain, it might be rational to displace, by whatever method, one emotion within one's psychological set with another. But for someone who already has a child and who loves that child, it is difficult to see by what psychological route one comes to the thought that it would *now* be better not to have to suffer even the extreme anxieties of virtually certain tragedy than to endure those anxieties as part of a life that includes loving one's child. It is, of course, in part trauma to these sensibilities that led to Sophie's collapse.

VII.

The extirpation therapists, then, need not hang out their shingles and expect loving parents to come knocking, even where there is a great deal of pain to be endured for the sake of the children. What all this shows, of course, is that loving parents are not hedonists, no matter how sophisticated that point of view is made to appear. As applied to loving parents and their vulnerabilities, Epicurean extirpation therapy simply falls prey to hedonism's age-old paradox: one must first value things other than pleasure to value the pleasure of those things. To be a loving parent, one must value a child's future welfare more, and considerably more, than one values avoiding the fear of dying too soon.

This kind of analysis extends outwardly in two directions. First, it extends to other kinds of fears, and second, it extends to other forms of caring besides parental love. Loving one's children generates not only the fears of either oneself or one's children dying too soon; it generates other anxieties as well. Will the children get in harm's way before they are able to take care of themselves? Will harm find them in spite of their best efforts to avoid it? Will "friends" of poor character mislead them into habits detrimental to their becoming good persons? Will they find good mates, mates who will love rather than abuse them? Will the current generation adequately plan for a future that leaves them with prospects for a meaningful life? Is the current public character one that will nurture the better angels of their nature instead of catering to the whims of their immaturity? These and a thousand other worries come with the territory bounded by parental love, and if there is enough bad luck, the loving parent will be crushed by fears realized. But to steal a thought from Mill and export it to another context: it is better to be Sophie fearful than an Epicurean fearless.

If this multiplicity of vulnerabilities comes with parental love, it comes no less with other forms of personal love. Loving people fear for the well-being of their friends, their families, and their communities. When death too soon or harm of whatever variety threatens, anxieties are piqued, and if the more serious harms are realized, integral stress will sooner or later reach its threshold.

Beyond this are the boundaries of our caring for those with whom we are not specially related, for those for whom we have sympathy and respect. Their lives and their deaths matter to us, and mattering they render us vulnerable to fears realized in horrifying events. Removing the capacity for horror at these tragedies can come only by extracting that which makes us what we want ourselves and others to be. Thus the devastating dangers of grief and sorrow are part of the life well lived for those who care, even if such a life is not hedonically best.

CHAPTER 8

The Possibilities of Therapy

Stoic Strategies

Extirpation therapy might seem at this point nothing less than silly. Even sillier might seem a method that aims not just at extirpating *some* emotions from our psychology but the complete emotional repertoire itself. On Nussbaum's reading of the Stoics, it is just this kind of radical approach that they had in mind. The goal of this chapter, then, is to consider the kinds of arguments Nussbaum attributes to the Stoics in defense of such radical extirpation. For, according to Nussbaum, the Stoics argued that despite the strongly counterintuitive and apparently silly suggestion that *all* emotions should be extirpated, such a therapy is both rational and consistent with what we value most in ourselves and others.

Without becoming too involved in the issue of whether the details of Nussbaum's interpretation of the Stoics are historically correct, I will consider the arguments she attributes to them and evaluate those arguments on their own merits. I do this because Nussbaum herself presents these arguments not just as interesting historical artifacts but as live candidates for philosophical debate. I am therefore more interested in how these arguments apply to our lives than I am about getting things absolutely right about the Stoics. Such an approach is not without its dangers. It might indeed miss something about how it is best for us to think about our lives by not getting things absolutely right about the Stoics. This fact duly noted, however, we might also miss something about how it is best to think about our lives by not taking due notice of how Nussbaum interprets the Stoics and how she finds them both interesting and promising. That Nussbaum's Stoics are influenced in their appearance and behavior by her philosophical genes does not trouble me. Indeed, it is one of the major reasons that I find them important. Hereafter, then, I will refer to Nussbaum's Stoics simply as the "Stoics."

I.

The Stoics should be understood as interested in constructing a psychology that is conducive to a life of flourishing for natural creatures like us. The general goal of therapy, then, is the construction of a psychology that leads to eudaimonia, a eudaimonized psychology, as it were. The therapeutic subject, however, is one that has an instantiated psychology in need of alteration. Moreover, we must, if we are to make sense of the Stoic project, attribute to the Stoics the belief that human psychologies are in general both very highly malleable and malleable in response to elements within any particular instantiated psychology. Both points regarding malleability are important: the first because Stoic therapy is radical in a sense that will become clearer shortly, and the second because Stoic therapy, unlike its Epicurean rival, must come through rational deliberation rather than through "brainwashing" or something of the sort.[1] What we need, then, in addition to a general understanding of the goal of therapy is both a general account of the psychology of the therapeutic subject and a general account of a eudaimonized psychology for natural creatures like us.

Beginning with the general account of the therapeutic subject: the features of that psychology must be noted. Contained within it are various elements, including those that can be roughly divided into cognitive elements, conative elements, and affective elements. We should be careful not to force more concretely specified psychological entities within some neat division of these categories. Emotions, beliefs, intellectual skills, feelings, moods, sensations, desires—all are psychological entities of various sorts. Yet they do not all fit neatly within any one of the three mentioned categories but sometimes span them. The therapeutic subject is one for whom there is some sort of problem arising from the way these elements are instantiated within a particular psychology that prevents the subject from living the life of eudaimonia. Unlike the Epicureans, the Stoics believed that it was not some subset of the emotions that was the source of the problem but the emotions themselves, along with the beliefs, desires, values, feelings, and moods that go with them.

Thus any particular therapeutic subject will have a psychology that has instantiated within it a menu containing a variety of repertoires, among which is a repertoire of emotions. It is a characteristic of some of these repertoires that the existence of items in some other repertoires depend on them. If parental love is included within the emotional repertoire of the therapeutic subject, for example, the desire repertoire of that subject will include the desire for the future well-being of the subject's children. Repertoires of beliefs, feelings, and moods might similarly be dependent on what is contained within the emotions repertoire. Moreover, patterns of psychological response might depend on the relationships between kinds of repertoires. Without a repertoire of intellectual skills, for example, it is difficult to see how there could be a motivational repertoire of anything other than the crudest sort, even if that. Thus patterns of psychological response might depend on how repertoires are functionally related. If some patterns of psychological response depend on the relationships between some repertoires, these patterns might be enhanced or diminished by adding or removing the relevant repertoires. Central to the Stoic diagnosis of the therapeutic subject is that it is the existence of the emotions repertoire within the menu profile that creates the subject's dysfunctional psychology. That is, the patterns of psychological response that disrupt the subject's life are a function of the fact that the menu contains an emotions repertoire. Eliminate this repertoire and you eliminate the objectionable patterns of psychological response that prevent good living.

A eudaimonized psychology, on the other hand, is one from which all the functional psychological capacities that produce objectionable patterns of psychological response have been expunged. The Stoic version of this psychology is one in which there is no emotions repertoire on the menu profile or any of the psychological functions attendant on there being such a repertoire.

More can be said than this, however, even for a general account. Suppose, for example, that we eliminated from a psychology any belief repertoire whatever? What kinds of psychological functions would be left, and what kinds of patterns of psychological response would be possible? For one thing, there would be no emotional responses, if emotions require beliefs as a part of their functional apparatus, as both the Epicureans and Stoics rightly maintained. There could be certain kinds of moods, I suppose, but they would lack intentionality. Perhaps there could be desires, but the repertoire would be very limited in content, maybe only those relating to appetites and itches. Eliminating beliefs, then, from a eudaimonized psychology is very difficult. Although this was a project of the ancient Skeptics, it does not seem very promising because the psychology that results seems too minimalist to be human. For one thing, it is difficult to see how to get any kind of agency out of such a psychology, unless we replace beliefs with something like quasi-beliefs, whatever those are.

An emotionless psychology, on the other hand, is the one the Stoics would have us construct. The issue then involves what psychological functions and attendant patterns of psychological response would be eliminated with the elimination of the emotions repertoire. There could be moods, but only of a limited sort. There could be lots of beliefs, but none of them would be relevant to our lives vis-à-vis their usual place in our emotions. There could be desires, but none of those generated by emotional attachment. Affective responses like feelings would be limited to rather primitive pleasures and pains. Thus, on the Stoics' vision of this psychology, it would be plentiful in its cognitive functions but rather minimalist in its affective and conative functions.

Historically juxtaposed, then, were two therapeutic strategies, the Skeptic strategy and the Stoic strategy. The first advocated a minimalist psychology without a belief repertoire as the psychology best for humans. Supposedly, humans are to be able to retain an extensive array of affective and conative repertoires without beliefs. On the Skeptic view, we can retain a rich emotional and affective life but remove the sting from it by getting rid of our beliefs, not just some of them but the whole repertoire (perhaps replaced by a repertoire of quasi-beliefs). That this is even a coherent view of a possible psychology is highly questionable. The intentional structure of emotions seems to require beliefs (real, not quasi-beliefs) as part of that structure. Nor do things fare better for motives: what is it to have a motivational set without any beliefs? Perhaps Nussbaum's comparatively short treatment of the Skeptics reflects a similar pessimism on her part regarding this therapeutic model. Nor does Annas find the project ultimately coherent.[2]

In contrast to the Skeptics, the Stoics advocated a psychology allegedly rich in cognitive functions but very minimalist in affective and conative functions. Emotions are to play no role in the Stoic vision of the good life, and desires only a minimal role. But like the Skeptic view, there are deep questions about the coherence of such a psychology, especially regarding whether it would contain a motivational repertoire at all. The problem for the Stoics is not like that of the Skeptics regarding motives. The Stoics would provide a belief repertoire. Their problem is providing the essential affective features of motivation. We will come back to this. What is important here is that we see why they thought that a eudaimonized psychology would expunge the emotions repertoire with all the psychological implications for other components of our psychologies.

The best life for humans, according to the Stoics, is the untroubled life, and the untroubled life is the life of virtue. Although specifying the conceptual relationship between the untroubled life and the life of virtue is difficult, I take it to be something like the following: the best life is valued for its intrinsic qualities, and virtuousness is an intrinsic quality of that life; moreover, virtuousness is valued for its intrinsic qualities, and untroubledness is an intrinsic quality of it. I do not take the Stoics to believe either that the virtuous life is only instrumentally valuable as a means to the untroubled life or that the untroubled life is only instrumentally valuable as a means to the virtuous life. Rather it seems best to understand the Stoics as valuing the untroubled life because they believe that such a life is an intrinsic quality of the life of virtue. One rather radical claim of the Stoics is that the life of eudaimonia *is identical to* the life of virtue. It would not follow from this, however, that the life of eudaimonia is identical to the untroubled life, for there might be other ways of life that have untroubledness as an intrinsic quality.

What does follow from this radical thesis, however, is that nothing external to virtue is intrinsically important to a life well lived. Furthermore, the Stoics believed that the virtuous life is sufficient to itself. Attaching oneself to what they called "externals," things external to virtue, not only does not add to a life of eudaimonia; it undermines such a life. It reflects a commitment to things external to the intrinsic qualities of a good life whereby troubledness can enter into a life. Moreover, if untroubledness is an intrinsic quality of virtuousness and thereby of a good life, we can conclude that any psychological source of troubledness is not rooted in either virtue or a life well lived. It is a short step from here to the radical prescription of extirpating the emotions repertoire. All that is needed is that an emotions repertoire of any significance attaches importance to externals in a way that facilitates troubledness as a pattern of psychological response.

Positive emotions attach intrinsic value to their intentional objects, but the intentional objects of emotions are not a part of virtue; they are external to it. Even if being a loving parent is a virtue, one's child—the object of one's love—is not a part of that virtue. Thus the Stoics found themselves in the odd position of maintaining that the virtues that seem to require emotions do not. Their views on friendship are remarkable in this regard. They thought of friendship as a virtue but as having a nonemotional source. Grief over lost friends was criticized as showing improper attachment to externals; still one was to value one's friends both deeply and yet not in a way that facilitated troubledness as a pattern of psychological response to tragedy should it befall them. Just what this deep valuing that is immune to such patterns of response is supposed to be is, as far as I can tell, utterly mysterious. I will leave this issue to those who find the Stoic project more promising than I to work out. Nevertheless, it seems that Nussbaum is right to interpret the Stoics as advocating the extirpation of emotions in this radical way because the Stoics did insist that the emotions attach the person having them to externals, which is a denial of the self-sufficiency of virtue on their view.[3]

For those who doubt that the Stoics were advocating a radical approach to the extirpation of the emotions, several things can be said. First, any interpretation of the Stoics must show that they are critics of Aristotle and that they offer a philosophical alternative that is intended as a replacement of Aristotelianism. In this way, an adequate interpretation of the Stoics must show that they are in the historical lineage of both Epicureanism and Skepticism as competing reactions against Aristotle. How these Hellenistic schools differed, then, from Aristotle and from each other is crucial. Anyone doubting that the philosophical climate was fertile for radical alternatives need only look to the Skeptics for a clear example. Indeed, it seems that the Skeptics were more radical in some ways in their reaction to Aristotelianism than either the Epicureans or the Stoics. Moreover, it seems that one of the features of Hellenistic ethics in general that distinguishes it from Aristotelian ethics is its rejection of the view that eudaimonia can come through anything but radical measures. With this they all agree that Aristotle is just too conservative and trusting of ordinary experience.

In this regard Annas says,

> Ancient theories are all more or less revisionary, and some of them are highly counter-intuitive. They give an account of happiness which, if baldly presented to a nonphilosopher without any of the supporting arguments, sounds wrong, even absurd. This consequence is frequently evaded because it is assumed that ancient ethical theories are morally conservative, concerned to respect and justify ancient ethical intuitions without criticizing or trying to improve them. . . . [A]ll the ancient theories greatly expand and modify the ordinary nonphilosophical understanding of happiness, opening themselves to criticism from nonphilosophers on this score.[4]

When the Epicureans say that more of a good life is not a good thing, when the Skeptics say that we should suspend belief in regard to any proposition whatever (even the Skeptic's thesis), and when the Stoics advocate extirpating the emotions, they are expressing a deep-seated rejection of Aristotelian optimism about ordinary experience. Consequently, attempts to understand these schools of thought in terms of a less than radical accommodation of our ordinary beliefs about the good life simply fail to read the historical trends of philosophical development in the ancient world.

More specifically, the Stoic thesis that the life of eudaimonia *is identical to* the life of virtue is a radical departure from both Aristotle and other Hellenistic departures from him. Only the Stoics claim that the good life is identical to the life of virtue, but all the Hellenistic schools are motivated by a stronger commitment to self-sufficiency than is found in Aristotle. At its core, the debate among the Hellenistic alternatives seems best understood as a debate that just is about what kind of theory can best accommodate the self-sufficiency of a life well lived. It is the thesis that the life of virtue is identical to the good life and that untroubledness is an intrinsic quality of virtuousness that is intended to secure the best account of self-sufficiency. And *this* thesis *is* incompatible with anything other than a radical departure from Aristotle, as well as, though in different ways, from Epicureanism and Skepticism. In fact, it seems that the most distinguishing feature of Stoicism as a moral theory, ancient or modern, is its radical interpretation of the moral importance of self-sufficiency. Care about self-sufficiency enough and radical thoughts, among them Stoic thoughts, will soon follow.

But why care about self-sufficiency so much? There are both historical and philosophical elements to an adequate answer to this question. Historically, one should keep in mind the place of philosophers in political life from the trial and death of Socrates to Seneca's suicide. It was increasingly difficult to believe in the prospects for the public success of virtue. Moreover, it was increasingly difficult to expect public success as a function of virtue. Thus if one was to believe that there was a connection between the virtuous life and the life well lived, it was difficult to believe that the connection had anything to do with the public success of virtue. Virtue, then, became increasingly not only its own reward but the only reward. Being troubled about the public failure of virtue became just another concern for externals to be extirpated. Not to be extirpated, however, was the purely rational commitment to the obligations dictated by the virtues. This included the commitment not only to friendship, family, and country but also to humanity itself. Thus by the time we get to Seneca, we have a thinker who wants to endorse a theory that extols the virtues of friendship but without emotion, especially those emotional attachments that can lead to grief. We also have a man who can take his own life, not out of despair, but as a rational repudiation of both Nero and the emotional self-indulgence with which his era was associated. Seneca's life aimed at and his suicide expressed from his point of view the superiority of self-sufficiency over emotional indulgence.

Viewed in this light, Stoic extirpation therapy looks no more implausible than the ideal of self-sufficiency that drives it. But there are *philosophical* ways of motivating the ideal of self-sufficiency that strategically address the counterintuitiveness of the radical claim that we should remove the emotions repertoire from our psychological menu. With this we turn to the philosophical defense of what seems an extremely implausible radicalism.

II.

Among the Stoics, Nussbaum finds three kinds of arguments for radical extirpation against Aristotelian moderation of the emotions. She identifies them as the motivational argument, the argument from excess, and the argument from integrity.

The motivational argument takes the form of denying that we need the emotions and desires generated by them to account for the commitments of friendship, family, community, or to humanity itself. Reason, it is claimed, is sufficient for these ends. Thus extirpating the emotions is not supposed to have the result that we do not have obligations to our friends, our families, our communities, and humanity. If successful, this would reduce the counterintuitiveness of the original thesis that we should extirpate the emotions repertoire. Also, it is consistent with a set of texts that seeks both to disparage emotional vulnerability through grief over lost loved ones and, nonetheless, to extol the virtues commonly associated with emotional attachments.

There is, however, no sophisticated treatment of the issue so central to Kantian worries about how reason can motivate independent of desire. A solution seems more to be assumed than argued for. Therefore, there is little I can say that I have not already said in response to the Kantian position on these matters in chapters 4 through 7. I will say, however, that the Stoics put an even greater emphasis on reason than did Kant. Kant would not have us extirpate the emotions but simply put them under the control of reason. The Stoics wanted a much stronger version of self-sufficiency, one that removed the causal efficacy of the emotions altogether.

The argument from excess is, I believe, the strongest of the three arguments for extirpation because it forces us to think deeply about our moral values. It employs moral arguments against the emotions and appeals to our sense of what we owe ourselves and others. Its general form is something like the following: (i) For any substantial emotional repertoire, E, and any psychology, P, it is morally permissible to instantiate E within P only if E does not have as one of its psychological functions a pattern of excessive psychological response that is contrary to our obligations to ourselves and others; (ii) there is no substantial emotional repertoire, E, that does not enable such patterns of excessive psychological response; (iii) therefore, there is no substantial emotional repertoire to be instantiated within any morally permissible psychology.

Nussbaum's description of Chrysippus's strategy can be taken to involve this argument. Chrysippus believed that Stoic therapy began with the therapeutic subject's conception of the good and led rationally to the extirpation of the emotions. A kind of reductio strategy, then, is available on this view to Stoic practitioners. For any patient's conception of the good, there are values according to which it is irrational to retain the emotions repertoire if it can be removed. This is true even for those who have strong reasons initially to value the emotions of personal love and the externals to which such emotions are attached.[5]

Like any general argument, however, the devil is in the details of how to establish it. Both premises can be challenged, but how successfully, of course, is determined by the arguments employed by the challengers. One might challenge the first premise by accepting the fact of excess as a function of any emotional repertoire, E, but denying that this is morally sufficient to disqualify instantiating E within P. One source of such a view might be the thought that the best that we can be is still not without flaws. What we are obligated to do and thus what is permissible for us to do is to construct our psychologies in the best way possible. Those who do not find the philosophy of mind behind Stoicism regarding motivational sources independent of emotion and desire plausible might find themselves taking this approach seriously. If I am not mistaken, this is the inclination of Nussbaum herself.[6]

It seems wiser, however, to resort to a denial of the first premise only after one has been forced to accept the second, that is, only after one has been forced to accept the fact of excess. Yet it is anything but clear that Nussbaum's analysis of the Stoics gives us sufficient reasons for doing so. Is moderation without excess possible? If the answer is yes, then the second premise is false. A precautionary note is in order, however. A sound inquiry in this regard should be open to at least three kinds of result: that inquiry will yield the conclusion that there is indeed objectionable excess; that inquiry will yield the conclusion that there need be no objectionable excess; and, finally, that what prereflectively looked like excess is in fact not objectionable after reflection. If either of the last two should prove the result of inquiry, then premise two is false. The third option simply recognizes the legitimate revisionary effects that inquiry can have on our pretheoretic intuitions.

III.

Nussbaum considers two cases of excess, one involving attachment to country and one involving romantic love, and both the dangerous effects of anger. It should be easy to see that uncontrolled anger can be both excessive and unjustifiable. Moreover, it should be easy to establish that such anger can be a function of other emotions, some of which we would extirpate if we could. The anger associated with jealousy is a good example. One reason we think jealousy is a bad thing is because it generates irrational anger that leads to harmful consequences. In addition, it is difficult to see what good such an emotion serves in mature people. If nothing good would be lost by removing jealousy and if something bad could be prevented by its removal, then why not extirpate it from the emotional repertoire? It would seem irrational not to do so if one could. This general line of thought seems to be the pattern of reasoning behind the extirpation of emotions in regard to their connections with excessive anger. The thought is that if you substitute other emotions of attachment for jealousy you get the same result. Call this rule for removing the bad without removing the good in regard to elements within a psychology the Principle of Extirpation. If the Stoics can succeed in giving a plausible analysis of a complete set of emotions that parallels this analysis of jealousy, they will have gone a long way in convincing us that what seemed counterintuitive turns out not to be after reflection. This must be kept in mind in the analysis that follows. I suspect, however, that for the pattern to have its initial appeal, we must not dwell too long on the fact that we readily find the extirpation of jealousy unobjectionable because we are quite confident that the extirpation of jealousy and the anger it generates can be done without extirpating the attachments of love. We probably believe that the best way to extirpate jealousy is by strengthening love rather than by removing it. But more on this later.

Nussbaum first considers anger in public service, and her analysis focuses on Seneca's *De Ira*. Beginning with a conception of what anger is that is shared both by Aristotle and the Stoics, the argument gleaned from her analysis seems to be something like the following:

The Stoic argument against anger:

1. Anger is the desire to punish or to return pain for pain to someone by whom one believes oneself to have been wronged.

2. As such, anger is a social artifact, a product of what we are taught to believe and judge, rather than an innate natural passion.

3. Anger is not necessary as a motive to any right action.

4. Virtue and duty alone provide motives for any right action.

5. Anger, as a social artifact, is a bad motivational force because it is unavoidably prone to exceed the boundaries of virtue and right action.

6. Anger is attached to externals through other emotions.

7. The externals to which anger is attached are not important, only virtue is.

8. Therefore, by the Principle of Extirpation—that we should extirpate any psychological element that threatens eudaimonia but adds nothing to it—we should extirpate not only anger but also any emotion or sentiment that feeds it.

Notice first that this argument incorporates both the motivational argument and the argument from excess. Premises 3 and 4 assert the existence of a motivational set that is independent of desire and sufficient for virtue. It seems to me that both these premises are false and that the best theory of practical reason we can produce gives us reasons for believing them to be false. Certainly if someone asserts that there are motives independent of the conatus of desire the burden is on them to establish the truth of these claims. One can insist on this, even if one does not identify motives with desires, as almost no one does. As long as the conatus of desire is an essential ingredient in motivation, both Stoicism and Kantianism have their difficulties.

For the moment, however, I will pass this by and focus on the other premises. Although premises 1 and 6 are, as far as I can tell, unobjectionable, they must be combined with premises 2, 5, and 7 to produce the argument from excess. Moreover, I cannot see that it is at all rational for creatures like us to accept *any* of them.

Not only is premise 2 (anger is a social artifact . . . rather than an innate natural passion) false, but the kinds of arguments attributed to the Stoics by Nussbaum do not establish premise 2, even if their premises are true.[7] To point out that we are not born angry and that conditions of scarcity can intensify anger to the point of excess does not establish that anger is not a natural innate capacity. Moreover, to point out that anger can be shaped in its behavioral manifestations by cultural heritage does not undermine its natural source. Think of hunger. We are probably not born hungry either, but conditions of scarcity regarding food will soon trigger hunger's mechanisms, no matter what society one happens to be born into. Further, if conditions of scarcity become extreme enough, there will soon be some rather fierce competition for food. Yet surely it is just silly to think that hunger is not a natural desire. To think that the fact that tastes in food vary from culture to culture establishes that hunger is a social artifact seems the shallowest form of social constructionism. What does seem sometimes to be a social artifact is the overall place of anger within a psychology. This is an important truth—one that is consistent with whatever is true in social constructionism—but it does not establish the truth of premise 2.

But what about premise 5, the one on which the argument from excess centrally hangs? It asserts that anger is a bad motivational force because it is unavoidably prone to exceed the boundaries of virtue. Here Nussbaum presents three examples of her own regarding anger in public life and uses them to both establish the plausibility of the Stoic argument and to illustrate its limitations. The first two examples are designed to lend credibility to extirpation, but the third limits its plausibility. I will consider each of her examples and argue that none of them lends credibility to premise 5.

Nussbaum gives the following statement of the first example.

1. An American platoon enters a Vietnamese village, looking for hidden Viet Cong soldiers, helpers, supplies. When the inhabitants of the village refuse to cooperate, the commanding officer, enraged at the "gooks" who are, to him, all enemies and not fully human, orders his men to open fire. Coming after months of frustration and suffering in the jungle, the invitation to revenge is delightful. Anger floods over them, sweet as a reward. They shoot children and old men. Women they rape and mutilate first. Finally they set the huts on fire, leaving nothing behind them. (This sort of story is told with reluctance by officers who know it as a communal nightmare that philosophy, at West Point, has not managed to exorcize.)[8]

Whether this describes accurately the actual events surrounding the massacre for which Lt. William Calley was convicted need not concern us very much. For example, that such rage is experienced as sweet is not clear, at least to me. That it was unjustified in Calley's case is. The problem I see with the example is that it does not establish premise 5; indeed, it seems to undermine it. The reason it undermines it is that Calley and his platoon were exceptions, how exceptional is unclear, but exceptional nonetheless. Are we then to imagine that the rule was that the other platoons did not get angry about the villagers and their cooperation with the enemy? Or is it more plausible that they were just as frustrated, just as confused, and just as angry, but more controlled in their response?[9] If controlled response was the norm rather than the exception, then this suggests that not only is there a psychology in which anger can be instantiated without excess but that even in these extreme circumstances it is statistically *likely* to be the psychology of a well-trained soldier. Perhaps West Point is doing a better job than some have thought.

To be sure, there is the issue of the exceptions, but what were they like, and what were the conditions like? The dispositions to kill old men and children and to rape and mutilate women are extreme dispositions, and so, by the way, are the dispositions to kill and maim adult males. What is it that encoded such dispositions within the psychologies of Calley and his soldiers? Whatever we say about these soldiers, we must realize that their victims were often either the enemy or indistinguishable from the enemy. Villagers—children, old men, and women alike—were dangerous just for this reason. But why did Calley's platoon respond in a way that was not the norm to these threats? Is it plausible to think that Calley's platoon and other platoons that responded with restraint brought the same set of dispositions to the battlefield in the first place? Given the facts of conscription, the likelihood that there would be platoons with enough individuals in them with antecedent asocial attitudes ripe for the excesses of war is extremely high. And given that the norm of response was not this extreme, we are led by this example toward the statistical probability of a psychology in which anger is instantiated as a controlled response even to extreme pressures.

Now to Nussbaum's second example.

2. As the fighting in the Gulf nears its conclusion, which is presented to the American people as an occasion of immense pride and satisfaction, General Norman Schwarzkopf appears on the news to discuss new evidence regarding the torture of civilians in Kuwait. (I tell this story, remembering how I heard him on the radio in my car, somewhere between Providence and Attle-

boro.) He speaks with contagious anger in his voice. He says that he does not know how to speak about people who did these horrible acts. He can only say that, whatever they are, they do not seem to be of the human species that we know and recognize.[10]

The excess of anger in question here is that excess that moves us to dehumanize others so that we can get on with extreme measures, the bloody business of war.

Before I respond to this example, I want to give Nussbaum's third example, because part of my response to the second is that it is not as easy as Nussbaum seems to think to distinguish the second and third examples, at least if they are to succeed in their points.

The third example is the following:

> 3. The colonel who heads the West Point philosophy department now tells a story that was told to them by Elie Wiesel on a visit to the academy a few weeks before. Wiesel was a child in one of the Nazi death camps. On the day the allied forces arrived, the first member of the liberating army he saw was a very large black officer. Walking into the camp and seeing what was there to be seen, this man began to curse, shouting at the top of his voice. As the child Wiesel watched, he went on shouting and cursing for a very long time. And the child Wiesel thought, watching him, now humanity has come back. Now, with that anger, humanity has come back.[11]

The point of Nussbaum's third example, I take it, is to establish some kind of limiting case against the Stoics and the complete extirpation of anger. Not to have anger, the desire to punish and to return pain for pain, in response to the kind of mistreatment of fellow humans as took place in the Nazi death camps is actually to have lost contact with humanity. It is for this reason that the black soldier's anger brought humanity back from where it had left.

What is it that makes such anger appropriate? If we take Wiesel's story as a guide, it is the inhumanity of the perpetrators. Thus anger of this sort is reserved only for those people who have become *inhuman*. And the unadulterated fact is that you cannot be a Nazi at heart and have much humanity left. So to be a Nazi, that is, a Nazi at heart, is to be inhuman. That is why the Nazis are the enemy and are to be viewed as such. Not to think of them as the enemy, not to think of them as fitting objects of anger, not to think of them as deserving of punishment and pain for pain inflicted, and not to think of them as less than human is to signal a loss of one's own humanity. This we learn from Wiesel's story.

So the difference between Schwarzkopf and Wiesel's soldier cannot be that Schwarzkopf reduced the enemy to the level of the inhuman and

Wiesel's soldier did not. Nor can it be that Schwarzkopf was part of a wholesale slaughter of the enemy and Wiesel's soldier was not. To get to the camps American soldiers first had to fight the Battle of the Bulge, and the road to Berlin was much bloodier than either anything in the Gulf War or anything that occurred between Hanoi and Saigon. These facts should not be swept under the rug of academic niceties. It was necessary to travel the roads from Normandy to Berlin to dispatch those inhuman bastards in Berlin. So if we vividly imagine the anger of Wiesel's soldier we must not overlook the fact that it had blood in mind. Surely he did not think the most adequate expression of his anger was just a good cursing. Perhaps he was looking back during his rage on past encounters with an enemy now more despised. In fact, it seems that our approval of the soldier's anger reflects our belief that one is not normally justified in going to war unless one is quite confident that the enemy has become less than human.

If we are to praise the anger of Wiesel's soldier and condemn Schwarzkopf, then, we must look elsewhere. We might simply believe that the former was justified but the latter was not. We might believe that the Iraqi regime was not inhuman and that Schwarzkopf was just exploiting the situation for some reason. In this regard, we can imagine Schwarzkopf in at least two ways: as a leader with a trigger-happy temper ready to dehumanize anyone who gives him the opportunity to display his macho; or as someone who believes the war is justified because some people are being treated as far less than human by other people who have repeatedly displayed their inhumanity. If we imagine him as the former, then surely he is unjustified in his anger and in his tendency to dehumanize others. Yet what is such anger a function of within his psychology so described? What we must imagine, in Nussbaum's own terms, is extracting the psychological elements that produce macho anger without extracting that which is a function of one's humanity in response to the inhumanity of others. Moreover, the evidence of what the Iraqi regime actually did both in Kuwait and in their own country leads one to the conclusion that they acted much like Nussbaum's rightly despised lieutenant in her first example, except with far less provocation. That this justifies the Gulf War is a far more complex issue. That it makes Schwarzkopf's anger the trigger-happy macho she rightly deplores is another.

What would we extract from Schwarzkopf's psychology as described as including macho anger? Surely nothing that would lead him to view as inhuman the behavior of people like the Nazis, the Calleys, and the

Iraqi regime of the Gulf War. Macho anger is not about the inhumanity of others. But where genuine concern for others resides, removing macho anger would leave intact the desire to punish and to return pain for pain to people of this sort. Without such anger, humanity cannot return where once it was. Those who are deeply attached to the well-being of others have very little psychological room for the trivialities of macho, but removing macho by adding concern for others does not lead in the direction of an emotionless psychology.

I cannot see, then, that the second example does any real work in establishing the truth of premise 5, that anger is unavoidably prone to excess. For every General Schwarzkopf and Patton, prone sometimes to brilliance and sometimes to petulance, there are at least several General Powells and Eisenhowers, military leaders whose anger motivates but with controlled efficiency and measured moral response. And sometimes that measure is extreme, very extreme. It was, after all, Eisenhower who set Patton loose across Europe, and without Eisenhower's leadership, Patton himself would have been far less a threat to Nazi survival than he was. Both men knew that they were dealing with an enemy that could withstand any barrage of mere profanity screamed in their direction. What it would take to bring this enemy to its knees was blood and lots of it. Thus if we admire the anger of Wiesel's soldier, we have to admire the kind of anger that is unflinching in the face of intransigent inhumanity.

Should we, then, be slow to public anger? The answer depends, I believe, on what we are angry about. We should be slow to view others as inhuman, but it should not be beyond the pale of our capacities. The world would be a better place if there were a lot less macho anger but a lot more anger at inhuman character. Perhaps what we need is a sense of anger that is more rather than less developed. Its connections to caring about others in terms of respect, sympathy, and community should be more developed, and when these connections are developed, there will be far less anger of the macho variety. Yet this is a clinical strategy that works in just the opposite direction of the one recommended by the Stoics. For it emphatically rejects both premise 5 and premise 7 (only virtue, not externals, is important) by resting its hopes on the value of caring about externals.[12]

IV.

I want to turn away now from Nussbaum's discussion of public anger to her discussion of anger and romantic love. The focus of her analysis is on *Medea,* one of Seneca's tragic plays. The issue is whether this play, sympathetically read, gives us good reasons for thinking that premise 5 of the previous argument is true as applied to anger generated by romantic love. That is, the issue is whether anger, as a function of romantic love, is a bad motivational force because it is unavoidably prone to exceed the boundaries of virtue and right action.

That horrible things have been done in the *name* of romantic love one can hardly deny. But few, if any, can compare with the deeds of Medea. Having been caused by Aphrodite to fall in love with Jason, hero and leader of the Argonauts, Medea's life is subsequently framed by crimes of passion. To facilitate Jason's escape from Colchis with the Golden Fleece, she killed her brother Absyrtus, scattering his limbs into the sea and thus retarding the progress of those in pursuit. Later, at Iolcus, where Jason was vying for the kingship with his uncle Pelias, Medea deceived Pelias's daughters into cutting him into pieces and boiling him. The fallout from this, however, prevented Jason from regaining his father's throne, and both he and Medea were forced to retreat to Corinth, where they lived together for several years and had two sons. Thus at this point in Medea's life her actions had brought two deaths and two births, all of which were the result of her love for Jason, but still there was no kingship. Apparently to secure his position with King Creon, Jason resolved to end his marriage with Medea and to marry Creusa, Creon's daughter. This betrayal came as such a blow to Medea that she set about to get her revenge. Discovering from Jason's own mouth that his children were his "reason for living," she, with the perception of the Nazi officer in Sophie's case, decides to punish him by taking that which is central to his life, slaughtering his children, one before his very eyes.[13]

Both Seneca and Nussbaum see in this a story of the excesses of romantic love, for the anger and revenge of Medea are rooted in her love for Jason. Without this love, she would not have killed her own brother, would not have brought about the death of Jason's uncle, and most certainly would not have murdered her two sons whom she allegedly loved. Moreover, if Seneca and Nussbaum are right, there is a great deal of Medea in all of us on whom romantic love has any hold. How are we then to be both romantic lovers and persons of virtue?

That there is a great deal of Medea in all of us on whom romantic love has any hold seems to be controverted by the facts. Among persons who have been jilted, perhaps even worse than Medea, there appear to be few instances of infanticide. This suggests that it is indeed quite difficult to instantiate the disposition for such murderous acts within a psychology of a person who loves her brother and her children, no matter how much she loves her husband. When Aphrodite was creating the psychology of Medea, she might well have arranged for a kind of attachment to Jason that led to Medea's horrible deeds; but it is anything but clear that she encoded within that psychology any deep concern for others. Moreover, it is not even clear that she encoded anything like a deep concern for Jason. Rather what seems to have been instilled in her was a deep *need* for Jason. Neediness and love, however, are quite different psychological elements, as any person of any maturity knows. Finally, for the story to be psychologically coherent, we must understand the harm done to Jason to be an assault on a disposition toward his children that is diametrically opposed to that of Medea. Jason loves his children in a way that Medea does not; otherwise where is the revenge? For these reasons, I do not find the story even remotely plausible *if* the vice in question is anger that leads to behavior like Medea's. Most people simply do not abuse their romantic lovers in any extreme way when the relationship is broken. When they do, we suspect that it was not love that anchored their relationships in the first place.

Nussbaum, however, suggests a more modest thesis that might nonetheless confirm premise 5. We are like Medea, according to Nussbaum, because of what we might call ugly thoughts, and ugly thoughts are contrary to good character. Among the kinds of ugly thoughts she has in mind are the angry wishes and fantasies that come to us when our loving sentiments are assaulted. While it might not be true that most of us are psychologically constituted in such a way that we are even capable of responding to former lovers with the vengeful wrath of Medea, few of us are immune to having thoughts that imagine or wish for undue harms to come to those who have hurt either us or those we love. The thought here is to admit that Medea-like dispositions to actual behavior are not essential to the psychological instantiation of romantic love; but, by the same token, it is just naive to think that romantic love can find a place in a psychology without some disposition to ugly thoughts regarding those who violate our love. Passion generates heat, and this is one of the ways it will in fact burn if things go wrong, even for the best of lovers.

This line of thought, I believe, is more plausible and must be considered with some seriousness. It does in fact seem plausible that it is either impossible or, at least, highly unlikely that romantic love can be instantiated within a human psychology in a way that makes *no* place for such ugly thoughts. Less clear, however, are the implications of this.

To some extent, the implications turn on how extensive such thoughts would be in a psychology that both instantiated passionate commitment and minimized the disposition to such thoughts. One way in which the extent of such thoughts could be measured would be in terms of their content: what pain is wished on or fantasized about regarding the offender? We can consider two extremes: one where the pain wished on the offender marginally exceeds the pain of the offense and one where it is excessive in the Medea sort of way. If the pain wished for *fits* the offense, it hardly seems excessive.

The latter extreme hardly seems inevitable. What is the argument or clinical data that suggests that one cannot be deeply passionate without being disposed to *murderous* thoughts should things go wrong? We must keep in mind here also that a murderous thought might nonetheless be still only a marginal reaction. If the offense is great enough, the difference between taking the offender's life (not that of his or her children) and some other reaction might only be marginal. A lot would depend on how cases are described. Still, any adequate analysis will yield extreme cases.

Another way in which extent might be measured regarding ugly thoughts has less to do with content than pervasiveness. On the one hand, they might be ephemeral, dissipating almost as soon as they appear with little or no recurrence and thus occupying little space within a person's psychology. Or, on the other hand, they might be relatively permanent, festering and growing but stopping short of action. In the latter case, they fill a person's life and clearly prevent good living. Thus ugly thoughts can vary in extent from being ephemeral and marginally excessive in content to being recurrently pervasive and extreme in content.

Nussbaum, I believe, inherits the burden of showing that recurrent ugly thoughts of the extreme sort are essential, if she is to maintain that there is a great deal of Medea in all of us. I do not see that she has argued for this or that the Medea story lends any credibility to it.

Yet there remains the excess in between appropriate and very excessive anger, and this may be enough to establish premise 5 and evoke the Principle of Extirpation. Settling this issue, however, is not as easy as it might first appear.

It would make a difference, I believe, if the best psychology we could expect from instantiating romantic love of significant passion involved only dispositions to ephemeral and marginally ugly thoughts. There certainly is no reason to think that passion varies proportionately with the extent of excess regarding the disposition to ugly thoughts. Still it seems that if we allow *any* degree of such thoughts as essential to romantic love, it looks like premise 5 is true. That is, it looks like the anger generated by the best instantiation of romantic love we can provide is unavoidably prone to excess regarding the boundaries of virtue.

We seem to be faced, then, with a choice from among three alternatives. First, we might simply capitulate and accept the argument and the therapy. This is to take the route of pure Stoicism. Second, we might accept premise 5, reject premise 7 (that externals are unimportant), and swallow the fact that the best of human character involves some vice. This, I believe, is Nussbaum's choice and constitutes a rejection of pure Stoicism. Or third, we might, despite appearances to the contrary, reject the claim that the disposition to excess involved in ephemeral and moderately ugly thoughts is a vice.

Shortly I will argue for the third alternative, but first I want to address the second, the one I take to be Nussbaum's, for I consider it a very live candidate for endorsement. I indicated this earlier when discussing Kant, the concept of unqualified value, and human dignity. There I suggested that one reason for rejecting unqualified value as a basis for human dignity might be that we might not be able to instantiate virtues without thereby instantiating vices. If this is true, it might seem that both the first and the second alternatives are incompatible with my claim that some integral breakdowns are benign. The first because the source of integral breakdown on my view involves the emotional attachment to caring about, among other things, externals. The second because integral breakdowns would always involve some vice, even if virtue too was involved, and would thereby always be malignant rather than benign.

To conclude the latter, however, is a mistake. Even if it turns out that we should accept the second alternative, we should not reject the claim that some integral breakdown is benign. The reason we should not is that the fault lines of character are various. To assert that the best of good character involves vice is to assert that the integral threshold of good character has both malignant and benign fault lines, that our dignity, as we discussed earlier regarding Kant, is not predicated on unqualified value. It is to assert that some of the bad things about us are functions of what is good about us and that these bad functions render us vulnerable to malignant integral breakdown. Moreover, it is to assert that there is no avoiding this. It does not follow from this, however, that there is no benign integral breakdown. For even assuming the qualified value of human dignity and character, not all the integral thresholds that come with the virtues of caring break along the malignant fault lines.

Consider Sophie in this regard. It is difficult, and probably impossible, to imagine (in any substantive sense) Sophie as capable of Medea's anger. Nonetheless, it should not be difficult to imagine her as capable of ephemeral and moderately ugly thoughts. Yet it was not an assault on her capacities for such anger as embedded in her love for her children, her family, and Nathan that brought her down. It was the caring about their welfare, the desire to share their lives and affection, and the grief of their loss and misfortune that shattered her life. These fault lines are good and, as far as I can see, are good even if they are attached to modes of caring that have other fault lines with other values. So even if Nussbaum should be right about the second alternative, this is no reason to think that all integral breakdowns are malignant, or even merely nonvicious; some are benign, a function of what is good about us.

But we should not yet admit to the second alternative and consent to the view that the best of human character involves some vice. There are two reasons for this. For one thing, Nussbaum has not given a convincing case for that alternative, though she has given it considerable standing as a viable option. For another, the third alternative is at least as viable. Or so I believe.

How could ugly thoughts, however ephemeral and moderate, be anything other than indicative of vice? This seems to me a legitimate question, but one that has a plausible but complex answer.

Ugly thoughts, remember, are wishes or fantasies about undue punishment or pain coming to those who have harmed either us or those we care about. Surely, then, part of thinking this matter through involves some careful attention to what wishes and fantasies are and the values, good and bad, we place on these things. Nussbaum asserts, with apparent approval, the Stoic belief that wishing for something bad reflects as badly on us as actually doing something that is bad. On this view, there is no significant gap between ugly thoughts and reprehensible actions. Kant, on the other hand (also a person significantly influenced by the Stoics), said that there was a qualitative difference between wishing for the right thing and willing the right thing. I assume he would have thought the same thing regarding the difference between fantasizing about doing the right thing and willing the right thing. He did, however, think that there was no difference in the quality of the will that willed the ends of right action but failed for external reasons to accomplish those ends and the will that succeeded at those ends. What are we to say, then, that good wishes do not reflect virtue but bad wishes do reflect vice?

I think it depends on how we understand wishes. Here it seems reasonable to think that the analysis of good wishes and bad wishes should have a similar structure. Consider first the case of good wishes. Suppose I genuinely wish that I could help you. What would normally be the pattern of behavior that would reflect that this is a genuine wish, rather than just a fleeting thought? Usually, if I say that I wish that I could help you but cannot, there is some assumption that there is something that prevents me from helping. Either I do not have the means or the ability necessary to help you, or there is some greater value than helping you that I would have to transgress in order to help. Yet notice that if either of these is true, then removing the obstacle to helping, either by providing the means or ability to help or by eliminating the conflict of values, transforms the wish into a willingness to act. But if this is what a genuine wish is, it looks like Kant was just wrong about wishing not conferring any moral worth, because genuine wishes are connected to the will in very deep ways.

Another possibility is that Kant had in mind wishes that are not genuine wishes. Yet how do we tell a simulacrum of a wish from the genuine item? The answer seems clear: remove the obstacles and there is no willingness to act. Sometimes we discover about ourselves that we do not in fact wish for what we think we do, and we discover this when faced with free access to the objects of our alleged wishes. The same, of course, can be said for our fantasies. Do these simulacra of good wishes confer any moral worth on us? Here it seems to me that Kant is right; they do not, at least regarding those apparently good wishes that are ephemeral. Why? Because they are not sufficiently connected to the will to reflect on our character. Put another way, they are not sufficiently embedded in our character to affect the quality of our will. And it is important to understand that it is increasingly difficult to drive a wedge between good willing and merely apparent wishing as one moves away from merely ephemeral wishing simulacra toward genuine wishing. Thus it is difficult to see how this kind of wishing for the right thing is a virtue at all.

What seems odd, at first, is that on this view good wishes can be a function of a bad will and character. Can good wishes be a function of bad character? The answer is yes, if we confine ourselves to ephemeral wishing simulacra. They are a function of a psychology not fully functioning. There are enough of the elements within that psychology for good willing such that, as long as other elements of the psychology are not triggered, thoughts of, say, helping others, appear in consciousness as genuine wishes. But this is possible as long as thoughts about effort and sacrifice and such are eclipsed from view. Let any of these elements even begin to appear and the good wishes disappear. Is it possible to instantiate a bad character in such a way that it is always fully functioning? I suspect that the answer to that question is no, if bad character is rich enough in its elements. If this is true, we cannot have bad character of any significance without good wishes. Think in this regard about the psychological elements that allow for cruelty. Even cruel people have fleeting thoughts of good wishes due to the partially functioning mechanisms of their psychology. Yet we do not for this reason think that such good wishes reflect virtue. They are merely the transitory effects of a psychological system in a temporary state of partial functioning.

I cannot see what prevents an exactly parallel analysis of ephemeral, moderately ugly thoughts. Some ugly thoughts are genuine wishes; some are not. Some are simply ephemeral simulacra. Can bad wishes be a function of good character, and is it possible to instantiate a good character of any richness in a way that it is always fully functioning? If the fleeting good wishes of cruel character do not reflect virtue and are merely the function of a psychological system not fully functioning, then fleeting, moderately ugly thoughts are not vices, even if they are a function of the partial functioning of a good character. Those who genuinely love their loved ones do not genuinely wish them harm, when that love is instantiated in an otherwise good character. Still even these lovers are subject to some kinds of ugly thoughts. Of course, genuine love is not always instantiated within an otherwise good character. But, then, when ugly thoughts and genuinely bad wishes emerge from these other sources, they are indeed vices, but they are not the vices of love.

Finally on this score, it seems plausible that, often at least, the ugly thoughts that appear as a result of the partial functioning of a psychological system appear *as ugly* only when other parts of the system begin to function. Suppose, for example, that my lover leaves me for another. In my stress, stress that impairs my ability to function psychologically at peak relative to my well-being, I unreflectively envision my lover in the embrace of her new lover. What I see is abandonment, betrayal. I have not yet separated myself psychologically from a way of viewing my lover in such way that allows me to take this picture as anything other than betrayal *unless* I am able to reflect on it. My immediate thought, then, is betrayal, and my anger seems fitting: pain appropriate to the pain inflicted. When reflection comes in, however, I see, assuming this to be true, that my lover did not betray me, but our relationship simply came to an end for her, despite her best efforts to preserve it. Realizing this, I see my immediate response as ugly and feel badly for it. With a little more reflection, I realize that these thoughts do not reflect badly on me unless they persist and fester to become more than they are now.

V.

Thus it seems very plausible that the third alternative is preferable to the other two. That is, it is plausible that we should reject the claim that the disposition to excess involved in ephemeral and moderately ugly thoughts is a vice. If this is true, then premise 5 as it relates to romantic love is false. Nor should it be difficult to transfer this analysis to other forms of attachment to externals and thus avoid both premise 5 regarding excess and the view that externals are not important. If this is true, then the argument from excess is defeated. Moreover, insofar as the argument from integrity involves the claim that emotional attachments undermine integrity by leading an agent beyond the bounds of good character, it too is defeated.

It is important to realize, however, that the maturity that comes with avoiding excess does not bring with it invulnerability to integral breakdown. Although it should be noted that such maturity does require that one integrate one's commitments and attachments in such a way that lessens vulnerability. Nevertheless, the kind of invulnerability that such maturity brings is invulnerability to malignant rather than benign breakdown. If we are capable of developing our psychologies in such a way that ugly thoughts are limited to the ephemeral sort, we can reduce our vulnerability to integral breakdown due to excessive anger. If we cannot, we remain subject to malignant breakdown. When it comes to Medea, we see someone consumed by anger generated by vice, and one does not have to be a Stoic to think so. With Sophie, however, it is difficult to see how her stress is to be understood as a function of ugly thoughts. Whether it is romantic love, parental love, friendship, community bonding, or impartial sympathy and respect, emotions of care, however moderated within a eudaimonized psychology, are not immune to the threat of tragedy even to the best of people, and no amount of virtue can change this fact. As Aristotle said, for a good life, as well as a good character, one needs a modicum of good luck.

CHAPTER 9

Troubledness and Strength of Character

Thus far I have been arguing against viewing character and what is good about us as involving the kind of strength that the Stoics and Kantians believe the best of persons to have. Nevertheless, it would be a mistake to think that the view that some integral breakdown is benign marginalizes the importance of strength of character. It is one of the crises of our day that so little emphasis is put on strength of character in dealing with life's adversities. To be sure, we should try to arrange society in a way that does not require the constant exercise of exceptionally heroic virtues. Yet some seem to believe that if we were to arrange society in just the right way, there would be virtually no need for character. Others, taking their cue from this group, seem to think that if society were arranged in such a way that any *significant* need for strength of character were required for living a good life, then this would be a sign that society is unjust. Thus any aspect of life that requires strong character signifies to them that they are *victims* of oppression.[1] The facts being what they inevitably are about the necessity for good character, they live their lives in resentment. Against this background of morally indulgent self-pity, Stoicism seems almost refreshing.

What we need is a conception of strength of character that avoids both the indulgence of self-pity and the myth of Stoic self-sufficiency as a response to life's troubles. I want to pursue some thoughts here about the concepts of troubledness and untroubledness that might provide some direction. I will suggest an interpretation of what troubledness might be seen as coming to and suggest two conceptions of strength of character that are designed as responses to troubledness so interpreted.

How, then, should we understand what troubledness is such that strength of character is a response to it? I suggest that we understand troubledness as integral stress in just the sense in which I have been using that concept throughout this book. One advantage to such an interpretation is that it will help us to avoid the problem of collapsing the Stoic alternative into some form of hedonism. To avoid troubledness is not simply to maximize the avoidance of unpleasantness or even misery quantitatively measured. It is to avoid the kind of psychological forces that threaten the breakdown of personality and the categorical qualities of our psychologies. It is to avoid the kind of stress that threatens integral breakdown.

There are two other advantages of this interpretation as well. The second advantage is that it provides some way of understanding the Stoic claim that untroubledness is "natural" for creatures like us. It seems true that it is the nature of psychological systems to respond to integral stress in a way that is designed to reduce the stress. The response seems to be to seek the most efficient balance available within the system to reduce the stress and to restore as much harmony as possible between the system itself and the environment in which it functions. In this rather abstract sense, untroubledness does seem to be the telos of any adequately functioning psychology, even if it is not the intentional object of any state of consciousness.

Finally, the third advantage of understanding troubledness as integral stress is that it provides an empirical test for how adequate any prescribed psychology and any therapeutic model for dealing with life's troubles is for creatures like us. On this view, something must count as evidence that a therapeutic model for dealing with integral stress is a failure. This evidence involves the behavioral manifestations of integral stress and integral breakdown. Thus, if repeating ten verses from the Bible for ten straight days is prescribed as adequate therapy to reduce grief over a lost child to a manageable level, we can test the therapy by observing the ability of the patient to cope with the stress after ten days. If the behavioral manifestations of deep depression recur, we can draw some rather strong conclusions about the failure of the therapeutic model. Any therapeutic model should provide an adequate predictive model for its failure. On this interpretation, then, the concepts of troubledness and untroubledness not only play a role in the Stoic theory of value and philosophical psychology, they also play a role in moral epistemology.

With these advantages in mind, we can turn now to two conceptions of strength of character: one the Stoic model of self-sufficiency and the other a roughly Aristotelian model of a balanced emotional life. I begin, then, with the thought that strength is important, that good people are in fact strong people, and that they do not easily wilt before the troubles of life, either the onslaught of evil or the absurd turns of tragedy. But what is strength a function of in good people? Is it a function of their integrity? If so, then of what is their integrity a function? These are important questions to be answered by competing conceptions of strength of character.

According to both the Stoic model of self-sufficiency and the Aristotelian model of emotional integration, integrity can be seen as a function of one's character, where living one's life is a reflection of one's character. A good life is one lived in accordance with virtue, and a life lived out of accord with virtue lacks integrity. This can be seen as true on both views, despite the fact that the Aristotelians do not maintain, as do the Stoics, that the good life just is the life of virtue. Apparently, they disagree about what a good life is, because they disagree about what kind of character is *natural* to humans.

One way of understanding the Stoics' view of untroubledness as intrinsic to the best life for humans is that they view troubledness as unnatural. In a sense we have seen that this is true: integral stress signifies a psychology out of its natural balance. This way of seeing things establishes a fairly straight conceptual path from what is natural to what is a life well lived to what is virtuous. Virtue can only be a function of untroubledness, never a source of a troubled mind, because virtue is a function of what is natural for us and troubledness is unnatural. Moreover, anything that makes us vulnerable to troubledness cannot be a part of virtue. It becomes crucial, then, to understand virtue, and thus our integrity, as a function of invulnerability, as a function of something with unlimited strength. Were we to have enough of whatever is the basis for virtue, we simply would be invulnerable to troubledness, and our integrity would have no integral threshold. Like Kant, though long before him, the Stoics located this source of strength in the power of reason as a cognitive capacity that is at once both practical and transcendent of our affective and conative dimensions. Reason provides the strength that allows for untroubledness because it is self-sufficient for the good life, which is the life of virtue.

Self-sufficiency and untroubledness go hand in hand, not because reason provides strength to moderate emotions and desires, but because it removes any value we place on things that can give rise to being troubled. Reason provides strength, on this view, because it builds character out of a fabric that does not have an integral threshold since it is not vulnerable to integral stress. The strength of self-sufficiency, then, is the strength of total immunity, and it is again transcendent reason that is supposed to provide such immunity. The goal of therapy, on this model, is for the patient through the use of his or her own reason to gradually build his or her character out of one invulnerable cloth.

Unless we press hard on the concept of reason, all this seems quite coherent. Yet why does it seem so *unnatural?* Why should it be so difficult to give up our commitment to externals and the psychology that generates such concern if doing so is natural? Of course, it is possible that what is natural for us is much different than what we have been led to believe by society. Still one would think from previous comments that there should be something that counts as *evidence* that something either is or is not natural for us. At one level of explanation, breathing seems natural, because without oxygen we die. At another, our thumbs seem natural, because without them our evolutionary histories would have been much different. For similar reasons, sexual desire seems natural, because without it there seems no plausible reason to engage in those activities that propagate the species. At another level, social sentiments seem natural, because we seem simply to become psychologically unstable, even dysfunctional, when left to complete solitude.

The above examples include three kinds of explanation that seem to lend support to the claim that something either is or is not "natural." The first example involves a straightforward physical explanation: the function of oxygen in the blood, the sensitivity of the body to carbon dioxide buildup that triggers the need to exhale, and all of that. The second and third examples involve explanations in terms of natural selection. These explanations are harder to establish than the straightforward physical explanations of the first example. Nonetheless, well-formed evolutionary hypotheses are empirically testable; otherwise, they are useless except for their entertainment value. The third kind of explanation is psychological, and these too are often both difficult but nonetheless testable when well formulated. One would also think that for any psychological function of any species, there would be some physical explanation, some evolutionary explanation, and some psychological explanation for its natural standing. Yet it might turn out that regarding the natural standing of some particular psychological function there is some physical/evolutionary explanation that it is natural but some psychological explanation that it is "unnatural." In this way, something can be natural in one sense yet unnatural relative to its overall natural standing.

But what would such a psychological explanation regarding unnaturalness look like? It would seem that it would include some complex behavioral test relating to the organism's ability or inability to retain its integrity as the psychological whole it is in the context of its environment. If the protracted attempt to live a life of a certain sort with its psychological demands results in severe psychological dysfunction, then what evidence could be better than that psychology is unnatural? Put this way, it seems that troubledness in the form of integral stress just is the evidence for unnaturalness and that the Stoics were right. Yet if we understand the test this way and troubledness as psychological dysfunction of this sort, what is the evidence that the least troubled life is one without commitment to externals, one that *aims* at a life of self-sufficiency?

Indeed, it seems that the evidence runs in the other direction, that such a psychological project is self-defeating in some important sense. Aiming at self-sufficiency seems to fail due to the absence of a target. It might seem that striving for self-sufficiency is a clearly defined goal as long as we focus on particular projects involving dependency. Without self-respect, we seem overly dependent on others for self-approval. So we aim at remedying the deficiencies of character that lead to lack of self-respect, or alternatively at developing those traits that once attained allow us to view ourselves with respect and thus as less dependent. Thus in any concrete situation involving dependency the goal of self-sufficiency seems to make sense. But that self-sufficiency could be the very goal of life, let alone a life well lived, is anything but clearly coherent.

The same can be said of tranquillity, the conceptual cousin of untroubledness. What is it to seek tranquillity as the goal of one's life? We know what it is to seek some tranquillity *in* our lives when our lives are about something else. However, those who seek it for itself, whatever that would be, seem to have a very difficult time finding it. Those who do find a measure of tranquillity in their lives seem to find it as a result of caring about something else and by having things go reasonably well regarding those other things. Learning not to care as a way of being untroubled seems a very unnatural thing in just the relevant sense. Trying not to care about externals, about loved ones, about the quality of one's work, about the life prospects for others, just does not seem at all promising as a way to achieve tranquillity. Rather, it seems to lead, especially among those who seem to work hard at it, to a life of integral stress and troubledness of the deepest sort. Moreover, the dangers of detachment seem to lead less to tranquillity than to indifference, indifference that is often related to clear psychological dysfunction.

Yet the fact is that we do *not* care about tranquillity, even the absence of integral stress, in a way that makes it our goal to avoid integral stress in the most efficient way possible without regard to what else we care about. The fact is that the efficiency of a psychological system in terms of integral balance is determined by what values are encoded in the ways of caring internal to that system. Consider in this regard Robert Nozick's famous thought experiment involving an experience machine.[2]

Nozick's example of the experience machine was designed to show that we care about things other than the quality of our experiences. Even if there were a machine to which we could be attached that would give us any experience we want, we would not go on the machine if doing so came at the cost of our relationships and of actually doing something with our lives. Despite the fact that the imaginary machine could make us *believe* that our relationships were intact and that we were accomplishing all sorts of wonderful things, the fact that at the time of deciding to go on the machine we would know that our relationships were over and that we would never accomplish anything would prevent us from deciding to go on the machine. Except for people in the most dire circumstances, this seems absolutely right. But what does it show?

It shows that we are not hedonists: we care about externals, not just experiences. It also shows that we are not Stoics: we are willing to take on the stress that is involved in caring about externals. Moreover, if we extend the example to consider the kind of stress it would put on most of us if we were threatened with being forced to go on the machine, we would see that that stress would be enormous no matter how much tranquillity the machine promised to introduce into our lives once we were on the machine. If this is true, then it does not seem that a eudaimonized psychology would be one that extirpated concern for externals. And if this is true, it does not seem that a therapy that aims at self-sufficiency is at all plausible. Stoics might object that they would not go on the machine either, because doing so would not be consistent with a life of virtue, no matter what the quality of the experience while on the machine. This seems right to me, but it does not say anything about why *we* would not go on the machine. We would not do so because we care about externals, even in the light of fully general knowledge about the troubledness of a life committed to them.

Nor does it seem plausible that there is any credible evolutionary explanation for the natural selection of a Stoic psychology of self-sufficiency. In fact, given what we are like as a species and the environment in which we live, it seems highly likely that if our survival had to depend on the kind of reflectiveness embedded in Stoic rationality we would have been extinct millennia ago. This seems especially so considering the hunting/gathering environment in which our current genetic structure evolved. Self-sufficiency seems the last thing nature had in mind. Emotional attachment and the psychological interdependence that goes with it seem far more plausible. It is time now to see what kind of strength of character comes with such a view.

I have argued that caring about externals makes one vulnerable to integral breakdown, but it is important to understand that it is also caring that provides great strength against such dysfunction. How can something that makes one vulnerable to breakdown be a source of strength against it?

If tragedy should befall my children, I will survive it, if I survive it, not by means of practical reason, pure or otherwise. I will survive it because I care about others and they care about me. If tragedy befalling my children should rob me of my ability to care about others and to care about the quality of my work, then I simply will not survive. If tragedy should befall me regarding my ability to do my work well, I will survive it, if I survive it, because I love my daughters, my wife, my family, and my friends, and they love me. It is these modes of caring that allow me to cope with the integral stress that comes to other modes of caring and to cope with the tragedy that befalls the objects of these concerns. In this is our strength. Strip these modes of caring away and we become listless, not strong. Add tragedy to all at once, and breakdown is unavoidable for any person of good character.

Certainly, there are different kinds of persons we admire. Some care more about creativity than about other persons. Gauguin, for example, cared more for his art than his family. For him, perhaps, work could have carried him through family tragedy in a way that it could not have for Sophie. Perhaps there are even people we admire who care about things other than intimate relationships and yet they do have respect and sympathy for others. These people are not vulnerable to certain kinds of tragedies, namely, those that befall people who are involved in intimate relationships. However, they are not invulnerable to the tragedies that can befall a caring person. Had Gauguin lost his sight, integral stress would have assaulted him as deeply as it did Sophie. It is interesting in this regard that while Gauguin might look stronger than Sophie, he was probably just luckier. Had Gauguin lost his art, it is not clear that he

would have survived long at all. Sophie endured many tragedies before
succumbing to the stress, because the breadth of her caring gave her a
longer line of defense against tragedy. In neither case is there a person
who is invulnerable through lack of caring that we admire. Indeed, I cannot think of a single example of a person we would admire with such
Stoic invulnerability.

On the Aristotelian model of strength of character, good character is
made both strong and vulnerable by the same elements. The telos of a
psychological system that embeds the values indicative of the emotions of love, sympathy, and respect is an integral balance of the various
modes of caring. Instead of being cut from one invulnerable, self-sufficient piece of cloth, strength here is a function of a cloth woven from
different strands, individually and collectively vulnerable to integral
stress but nonetheless collectively very strong. This is a psychology of
great strength as well as great vulnerability. Does a notion of therapy
that aims not at self-sufficiency but at strength in caring seem plausible
in the light of empirical tests? Is there a plausible evolutionary story to
tell that favors it in natural selection? I think the answer to both is yes.

There is overwhelming evidence that those who cope best with
tragedy befalling loved ones are those who are involved in healthy personal relationships that are deeply intimate, even though it is this kind
of intimacy that made tragedy possible in the first place. This is not just
common sense; it is documented over and over again in the social sci-
ence literature.[3] Moreover, there is at least some evidence, in the case of
Seneca, that he did not cope at all well with the stress that came his way.[4]
Some will say that this is because being a Stoic is hard or that hypocrisy
does not refute an idea. Nonetheless, at some point this response is just
an avoidance of putting a therapy to any test.

A eudaimonized psychology on Aristotle's view is much more plausibly natural in terms of natural selection than is the Stoic version of self-
sufficiency. What is it that gives one, as a human organism, strength to
take an interest in life when one's health is poor and one is in chronic
pain? It is, in general, the capacity to care about externals. Without this
capacity, we would probably have given up the struggle long ago. Unlike
some other animals, we do not seem to take enough interest in simply
pursuing our appetites to give impetus to our lives. Moreover, it seems
that had nature not made us care intrinsically about others, it is unlikely
that merely prudential reasoning about narrow self-interest would have
preserved us. Nor does it seem plausible that had nature made us care
about others only in terms of respect and sympathy we would have cared

enough about living to survive. Perhaps this is why a psychology with a deep value for the intimacy of personal love was selected by nature as the psychology fitting us for survival. Perhaps it is why thoughts of a life with personal intimacy give us such strength against adversity and why thoughts of a life without it give us such troubledness of mind. And perhaps it is why good character is both like good diamonds and good wine.

Notes

CHAPTER 1

1. This does not contradict the previous sentence. For it might be that failures of strength always correlate with the absence of other good-making features of character.

2. See Immanuel Kant, *Groundwork of the Metaphysics of Morals,* trans. H. J. Paton (London: Harper Torchbooks, 1964), first chapter.

3. I develop in much more detail a conceptual apparatus for understanding the relevant features of a psychology that is vulnerable to stress in my manuscript, "Agent-centered Morality: Integrity and Human Agency."

4. Any natural kind will have at least three kinds of properties: intrinsic properties (what it is made of), structural properties (how the stuff it is made of is structured), and dispositional properties (its capacities for reacting when acted on). Hardness is a dispositional property of diamonds; moreover, a certain level of hardness is required of a stone before it *is* a diamond, even if it has the requisite intrinsic properties.

5. I am especially grateful to my colleague, Jim Harris, for discussion on this point.

6. Barbara Herman's views will receive special attention, as will those of Marcia Baron. See Barbara Herman, *The Practice of Moral Judgment* (Cambridge, Mass.: Harvard University Press, 1993), and Marcia Baron, *Kantian Ethics Almost Without Apology* (Ithaca: Cornell University Press, 1995).

7. I will focus especially on Martha Nussbaum's *The Therapy of Desire* (Princeton, N.J.: Princeton University Press, 1994) and Julia Annas's *The Morality of Happiness* (New York: Oxford University Press, 1993).

134 Notes to Pages 13–29

CHAPTER 2

1. The thesis is that necessarily virtues of care involve the possibility of benign integral breakdown. The analysis of cases confirms this thesis to the extent to which contrary analyses fail to accommodate both our value judgments and the relevant mental concepts. I know of no other way to defend the thesis.

2. According to Alcoholics Anonymous, temperance for an alcoholic involves the ability to live a life of total abstinence.

3. This formulation is not acceptable for rigorous analysis. It needs some general qualifier that rules out some commitments to loved ones as not being appropriate bases for positive evaluation of the agent. The point is that not all ways of being committed to a loved one are examples of loyalty, at least on any plausible conception of loyalty. For example, criticizing a loved one for being vicious to others is not a breach of loyalty on any plausible conception of loyalty to loved ones.

4. Marcia Baron argues that supererogation is not a defensible moral category and that it is best replaced with the Kantian notion of imperfect duties, properly understood. I do not know yet what I think of her arguments, but I take it that on Baron's view there is still room for the notion of exceptional virtue. If so, my point can be made without appeal to the notion of supererogation. She might, however, object that though there is exceptional virtue in some sense, there is no room for the distinction between malignant and nonvicious breakdown. At any rate, my thesis is that there are some breakdowns that are not preventable by the presence of a virtue, whether or not there is exceptional virtue. For Baron's views, see her *Kantian Ethics Almost Without Apology*.

5. For her discussion of supererogation in ancient moral philosophy, see Annas, *The Morality of Happiness*, 49, 115–116, 119–120, 120, n 240.

6. In this regard, the fact that we might not blame someone for lacking a virtue does not seem sufficient for our saying that the absence of that virtue is not a vice. Lawrence Blum has argued persuasively in his book, *Friendship, Altruism, and Morality* (London: Routledge & Kegan Paul, 1980), that depending on the background, we might not blame someone for being racist. But being racist is a vice, and it is the absence of the virtue of tolerance, among others.

7. I do not intend either the Schindler case or the Dahmer case to be about love, but to reflect credibility on the previous analysis of the soldier and thus on love and loyalty.

CHAPTER 3

1. See William Styron, *Sophie's Choice* (New York: Random House, 1976).

2. It is not clear that Kant's own theory yields that conclusion, but that is not the point here.

3. *Groundwork*, 65–66.

4. The suspicions of incoherence are along two lines, at least: one involving the coherence of noumenal selves and noumenal causality and the other involving motives without desires or sentiments. For discussion, see essays by Terence Irwin, "Morality and Personality: Kant and Green," Allen W. Wood,

"Kant's Compatibilism," and Jonathan Bennett, "Kant's Theory of Freedom," in *Self and Nature in Kant's Philosophy,* ed. Allen W. Wood (Ithaca: Cornell University Press, 1984); and Nicholas Rescher, "Noumenal Causality," in *Proceedings of the Third International Kant Congress,* ed. Lewis White Beck (New York: Humanities Press, 1972), 462–470.

5. One very radical thing about Kant's view is that he separates acting on principle from acting on sentiments. But even where we construe respect and sympathy as sentiments, we have seen that they do not have the structure to give us reasons for living. This point applies even more to principles. Principles cannot give us reasons for living. At most they can give us reasons for living one way rather than another. Moreover, the difficulty about living on principle applies on two major readings of Kant's notion of acting on principle. Consider the first view that we have a perfect duty not to commit suicide. On this view, the specific act of committing suicide is prohibited by the categorical imperative, and acting in accordance with this imperative has moral worth only when so acting is driven by the sense of duty as its primary motive. If we imagine someone whose life has lost its meaning, the requirement of acting on principle in this case becomes the requirement of living on principle. Now consider the more plausible view that acting on principle does not require a sense of duty as a primary motive but as a secondary motive, the motive to regulate one's life by the categorical imperative. The problem with this view for the person whose life has lost its meaning is that there seems nothing left to regulate. If such a person is to find reasons for living, it would seem that those reasons will have to be for the sake of principles alone. But it seems incoherent that one should find reasons for living in principles that are supposed to have as their function the regulation of one's reasons for living. See both Herman, *The Practice of Moral Judgment,* and Baron, *Kantian Ethics Almost Without Apology,* for defenses of the regulative role of principle in the moral life.

6. See Cicero, *De Amicitia,* XVI, 59–60.

7. I thank Keith Butler for bringing my attention to this last point.

8. For a discussion of Kant's reaction to romanticism, see Baron's *Kantian Ethics Almost Without Apology,* especially the last chapter, "Sympathy and Coldness in Kant's Ethics," pp. 194–229.

9. Speaking of Seneca and Kant, Marcia Baron says, "Both find something self-indulgent and self-serving in intense sadness for another. Seneca: 'Do you wish to know the reason for lamentations and excessive weeping? It is because we seek the proofs of our bereavement in our tears, and do not give way to sorrow, but merely parade it. . . . There is an element of self-seeking even in our sorrow' (Epistle LXIII, p. 431). Without pointedly suggesting that the sorrow is feigned, Kant suspects that many people content themselves with feeling sad for another. Priding themselves on their noble and intense feelings, they do nothing to help" (*Kantian Ethics Almost Without Apology,* 223–224). Later, she suggests that Kant's view is that care for another should make us vulnerable to sadness but only to the degree to which it aids us in discerning our duties to others and to the degree to which we can turn off the sadness when duty calls. Viewed in the light of Sophie's life, I cannot see that the above comments by both Seneca and Kant are anything but the most pious sermonizing. It certainly is the case

that we should train our sentiments to handle the expected losses that come in the course of a reasonably fortunate life. It is quite another to train our sentiments to handle exceptional tragedy, regardless of the contingencies of bad luck. To do the latter requires that we weaken them beyond recognition. To ignore this difference and to charge those who revere the sentiments with romanticism is to run the risk of making one's theory appealing only to the sanctimonious. To describe Sophie's response to the loss of her parents, to the loss of her children, and to the loss of her lover as self-seeking and self-indulgent is, to put it bluntly, crass nonsense. Later, in chapter 6, I will consider the stress experienced by the children of former Nazis. To deny that they should have had a sense of shame that could have been turned off in the way that Kant suggests on discovering what their parents did is not to imagine them as self-indulgent and self-seeking; it is to imagine them as people with good qualities under extreme stress, stress they should not, if they were good people, be able to turn off and on as duty requires.

10. There is a view something like this expressed by Seneca in regard to friendship. See Epistle IX and Epistle LXIII. Both are found in Michael Pakaluk, ed., *Other Selves: Philosophers on Friendship* (Indianapolis: Hackett, 1989), 117–128. As a Stoic, Seneca is worried about how friendship can be necessary to the good life and the good life be self-sufficient. Specifically, he is worried about grief. His advice, then, is not that one should not have friendships but that one should view friendship in such a way that grief is never the proper response to the loss of a friend. Supposedly, we are to extend this advice to all loving relationships. I cannot see that there is anything to recommend this view. As Annas points out in *The Morality of Happiness,* untroubledness is the final good for the Stoics. But they are committed to friendship being a part of the final good. These two factors combine to generate Seneca's implausible conception of friendship as being compatible with living an untroubled life. But neither friendship nor any other form of deep personal attachment is compatible with such a life. Moreover, friendship is worth more than its weight in trouble for those who are capable of it. I will come back to this in the chapter on Stoicism.

CHAPTER 4

1. I believe that any adequate account of moral experience must give an account of moral imperatives being categorical, but I do not believe that they have to be categorical in Kant's sense. Kant's sense requires that imperatives are both moral and categorical only if they are rational for all rational beings as such. This is to begin with the assumption that morality can be universal or nothing at all. I do not see that moral experience requires this. When we disapprove of the murderer, it seems to me we would disapprove of him even if murder was rational from his point of view all things considered. This is because the character of the murderer is such that the categorical commitments on which our character is based will not allow us to tolerate him, whether he is rational or not. Some of our sentiments are categorical features of our psychology, and this is why they command us categorically, even if they do not command others cate-

gorically. Nonetheless, some of these sentiments dictate how we judge other people. That these sentiments have such a role in our psychology is a contingent fact, but the directives of the sentiments are not contingent within the psychology.

2. It is not that desires and sentiments cannot play any role in practical reason but that their role is secondary or ancillary to something else. The complexities of their role need not concern us at this point.

3. See Herman, *The Practice of Moral Judgment,* for an excellent discussion of the concept of justification and pure practical reason in Kant. Another way to put the worry that both Kant and Herman have here is in terms of a distinction between justification and explanation. On the one hand, an occurrence has an explanation only if there is some set of antecedent causal conditions sufficient for its happening. On the other hand, an occurrence has a justification only if there is some set of reasons that require it but there is no set of antecedent causal conditions relevant to motivation that are necessary for its happening. For willings to be justified, then, they cannot depend on causes (involving motivational variables) but on reasons alone.

4. I will not offer an argument for this here. Compatibilists, those who believe that the denial of free will is compatible with responsibility, have their own reasons for rejecting the concept of pure practical reason. All my argument will establish, if successful, is that a refutation of the concept of pure practical reason is not in itself sufficient to undermine the notion of responsibility, even if free will is required for responsibility.

5. I believe this is basically Allen Wood's view. See his "The Emptiness of the Moral Will," *Monist* 73 (1989): 454–483, and his "Kant's Compatibilism," in *Self and Nature in Kant's Moral Philosophy,* 73–101.

6. I believe this, or something quite like it, is the view developed by Henry E. Allison in *Kant's Theory of Freedom* (Cambridge: Cambridge University Press, 1990).

7. See Herman, *The Practice of Moral Judgment,* 11, 14, 199, 201.

8. Marcia Baron expresses this worry in terms of what she calls the empiricist conception of motivation. See *Kantian Ethics Almost Without Apology,* 188–193. If my argument is sound, then we do not value the kind of freedom Kantians claim we do, which is not to say that we do not value free will on another conception. As Baron herself is concerned to argue, patterns of conduct more than individual actions are basic to moral judgment. It is one thing to say of a particular act that the agent could have acted otherwise. It is quite another to say that an agent could have chosen to be an unloving person, a person who does not have the dispositions of love and patterns of behavior in which love expresses itself. This is also true of respect and sympathy. What would be valuable about a person who could choose not to have the dispositions involved in respect and sympathy? Wouldn't this show that such a person was missing something? And, missing them, from what perspective would such a person choose them? We might very well value persons as agents in the following sense: if x is worthy of respect, then x is such that in a great many circumstances x could have acted other than the way x in fact acted. This does not show that we value persons as agents in the Kantian sense. What the Kantian needs to show is that we

value persons as agents in the sense that no matter what one's natural endowments in terms of inclinations one could choose to be either respectful or not, where being respectful is taking on a character that issues in a pattern of conduct. But I cannot see that we do value this. We would be perplexed at a person who could choose not to be respectful, not to be loving, not to be sympathetic, where these refer to basic elements of character. What I am asserting is that we do not value the power to create our character out of pure willing. This notion of the value of free will seems motivated more by a desire to be a god than to be responsible for one's actions.

9. I certainly do not take it that I have provided an argument for free will here or for the concept of volition necessary to it. What I have argued is that the relevant conception of volition is as open to a desire/sentiment standard of practical reason as it is to a pure practical reason standard.

10. Peter Railton has asserted that the Kantian charge against utilitarians to the effect that the latter do not treat persons as objects of respect is false. He claims rather that utilitarians simply have a different view of respect than the Kantians. I have some sympathy with Railton's objection in this regard, though I am not at all inclined to utilitarianism or consequentialism in any of its varieties. Kantians often speak as though they have a monopoly on the concept of respect, as though no other kind of theory is concerned to give respect a prominent status within a conception of morality. This is simply false, even though I know of no non-Kantian view that gives respect the kind of monopoly on moral status that the Kantian account gives. Still, it seems to me that utilitarians do not provide any crucial place for the concept of respect. But they do make a place for others as ends-in-themselves. This is because any sympathetic agent treats others as ends, not merely as means. The difference is that the concept of persons as ends-as-objects-of-sympathy need not include the concept of agency. For Kantians, persons are ends-as-agents, and as such they are objects of respect rather than sympathy. For Railton's views, see "Alienation, Consequentialism, and the Demands of Morality," reprinted in *Friendship: A Philosophical Reader,* ed. Neera Kapur Badhwar (Ithaca: Cornell University Press, 1993), 211–244.

11. I discuss in much detail the concept of regulative norms and their symmetrical functions in my manuscripts "Impartiality, Regulative Norms, and Practical Reason" and "Agent-centered Morality."

12. Kantians might argue that the categorical imperative and its procedures can generate direct duties of friendship. If so, what I have just said should make us suspicious of the Kantian claims regarding the relationship between the Kantian decision procedure and the concept of respect as a regulating function. In any event, Kantians must show us how the procedure generates these duties and what they are across a variety of practical contexts. I am not aware that they have.

13. This is true even of Robert Solomon's view that emotions are judgments. What he means by a judgment comes to more than simply being in a cognitive state, at least in the case of emotions. See Robert Solomon, *The Passions* (New York: Doubleday, 1976).

14. Of course, there are problems with understanding consciousness in purely natural terms, as well.

CHAPTER 5

1. See Herman, *The Practice of Moral Judgment*, 238.

2. See Thomas Hill, *Dignity and Practical Reason in Kant's Moral Theory* (Ithaca: Cornell University Press, 1992), 49.

3. This presupposes that there are no nonhuman rational beings that can be affected by the actions of others. If there turn out to be Martians that are rational and susceptible to being affected by the actions of others, they too will be moral subjects on Kant's view. Moreover, what our obligations to them are will be determined in part by contingent features of their being imperfectly rational beings, that is, beings that are rational but are also subject to the laws of cause and effect.

4. The modal operator has its place because Kant says, "*It is impossible to conceive* anything at all in the world, or even out of it, which can be taken as good without qualification, except a *good will*" (first emphasis mine; second, Kant's). From the *Groundwork*, 61.

5. See the *Groundwork*, 61–64.

6. Paul Davies has raised a question to me about whether there is a real difference between the logical consistency of the set of criteria, on the one hand, and the consistency of some set of traits falling under the application of those criteria, on the other. There is a difference, I believe, for the following reason. The test for consistency regarding the criteria as a set is whether there is *any* possible set of traits, such that if we did admire that set in a certain way, it could satisfy all the criteria. Suppose some possible sets of traits were single member sets. The problem of the consistency of the set of traits could not apply, but it would still seem to be an open question whether the set of criteria is consistent. That is, there could still be the issue of whether there is any single member set of traits that could satisfy all the criteria, and this does not seem to be an issue of the consistency of the set of traits but of the set of criteria.

7. Kantians will respond by insisting on a distinction between qualities of will and qualities of character. They will then argue that qualities of character might be exclusive in the sense worried over here but that qualities of will are not and that it is will, not character, that is unqualifiedly good. But since reservations regarding the distinction between qualities of will and qualities of character are even deeper than my reservations regarding this problem, the distinction does nothing for me in terms of a solution.

8. I would, however, give them the status of being moral subjects, that is, the status of being due direct moral concern. I reject the view that dignity, or the kind of dignity I believe humans have, is a necessary condition for being a moral subject.

9. Paul Davies has rightly pointed out to me that being an admirable agent on Nietzsche's view does essentially include vulnerability. However, I would question whether Nietzsche adequately accommodates the kind of vulnerability we admire in the most admirable people. Nonetheless, it does seem to me that Nietzsche is often closer to the mark in this regard than Kant.

10. Kantians will object that dignity status does not require effort, only a good will requires effort; dignity requires only the capacity for such an effort.

There are cases in which this seems right, namely, when the realization of capacities has been prevented by external sources or where those capacities have not yet developed to maturity. But where the capacities for dignity are there for use and are not used, I cannot see what is dignified about squandering them. What could be less dignified than that? But this is a topic for another occasion.

11. Christians here might point to the concept of the Incarnation as evidence that Christianity values imminence as well as transcendence. Perhaps so, but to the degree that the concept of the Incarnation is required to make sense of God's imminence and hence vulnerability to danger, Christianity admits both that transcendence is not an unqualified value and that such transcendence is foreign to the concept of dignity.

12. This distinction does a good deal of work in the *Critique of Practical Reason* in the argument concerning the existence of God as a postulate of pure practical reason. See Immanuel Kant, *Critique of Practical Reason,* trans. Lewis White Beck (Indianapolis: Bobbs-Merrill, 1956), 128–136.

CHAPTER 6

1. See Harry Frankfurt, "Freedom of the Will and the Concept of a Person," in his *The Importance of What We Care About* (New York: Cambridge University Press, 1988), 11–25.

2. See Pakaluk, *Other Selves,* 127–128.

3. This is especially true of Barbara Herman and Thomas Hill. But it is also true of Onora O'Neill in *Constructions of Reason: Explorations of Kant's Practical Philosophy* (Cambridge: Cambridge University Press, 1989) and of David Cummiskey in *Kantian Consequentialism* (Oxford: Oxford University Press, 1996). In fact, it is true of a generation of Kantians heavily influenced by John Rawls.

4. See *Groundwork,* 90–91.

5. I discuss the regulative relationships between respect and sympathy in much more detail in my manuscripts "Impartiality, Regulative Norms, and Practical Reason" and "Agent-centered Morality."

6. Marcia Baron suggests this role in the context of arguing against the moral worth of so-called overdetermined acts, acts that have more than one motivational source. See *Kantian Ethics Almost Without Apology,* 173–176. See also the last chapter.

7. Peter Sichrovsky, *Born Guilty,* trans. Jean Steinberg (New York: Basic Books, 1988).

8. There is another, more recent book in this regard. See Gerald Posner, *Hitler's Children* (New York: Random House, 1991). Posner's book differs from Sichrovsky's in that the interviews are anonymous in the latter but not in the former. What difference this makes as to the reliability of these reports is unclear. I tend to trust the anonymous interviews more, but both are revealing. Neither account is anything like a scientific study. Nonetheless, it would be decidedly unscientific to ignore the phenomena gathered in these accounts.

9. There is something of this in the psychology of being an American Southerner. I am a Southerner who loves the South and would without hesitation

describe myself as a Southerner. One of the things that makes this quite clear involves the fact that I experience so much shame regarding both my heritage and my contemporaries. No amount of achievements in literature, in music, in the contributions of Southern civil rights activists—such as Dr. King and Morris Dees—can erase the facts of slavery, the KKK, and the persistent bigotry among those William Faulkner called "red necks." Moreover, the fact that such bigotry exists elsewhere is utterly irrelevant to my feelings. I do, however, admit to being puzzled by Americans who claim to be horrified over the Vietnam War but who feel no shame regarding it just because they do not see themselves as responsible for it.

10. See chapter 3, note 9.

CHAPTER 7

1. See especially chapter 16 of *The Morality of Happiness,* 334–350, for Annas's account of the Epicureans and chapter 4 of *The Therapy of Desire,* 102–139, for Nussbaum's.

2. See Nussbaum, *The Therapy of Desire,* 201 ff.

3. Ibid., chap. 6.

4. For an interesting discussion along these lines see Bernard Williams, "The Makropulos Case: Reflections on the Tedium of Immortality,"in his *Problems of the Self* (Cambridge: Cambridge University Press, 1973), 82–101.

5. See Peter Unger, *Identity, Consciousness, and Value* (New York: Oxford University Press, 1990), and Bernard Williams, "The Self and the Future," *Philosophical Review* 79 (1970): 161–180.

CHAPTER 8

1. Nussbaum notes that an important difference between the Stoics and the Epicureans is the former's respect for rational autonomy and the latter's willingness to employ "cures" that ignore this value in humans. See particularly pp. 329–341 of *The Therapy of Desire.*

2. See Annas, *The Morality of Happiness,* 331–363.

3. Perhaps there is a way around this conclusion through the Stoic concept of "preferred indifferents." What the Stoics meant by this term is notoriously difficult to determine, either from textual evidence or from philosophical imagination. Somehow, preferred indifferents are externals that have worth (*axia*) but are not goods (*agatha*). I must admit to finding this utterly opaque. See Nussbaum's discussion in *The Therapy of Desire,* 360 ff. Annas tries to shed light on this concept in terms of what we would prefer in terms of "developed rationality," understood Stoically, but I cannot see what this comes to other than some form of opaque rational intuitionism. See *The Morality of Happiness,* 97, 122, 162, 167–168, 171, 307–309, 360, 389, 397, 402, 405–406, 409, 430, 432.

4. Annas, *The Morality of Happiness,* 331.

5. See Nussbaum, *The Therapy of Desire,* 318.

6. I take this to be the thrust of chapter 12, section VIII, of *The Therapy of Desire,* 480–483.

7. See Nussbaum, *The Therapy of Desire,* esp. pp. 410–426.

8. Ibid., 402.

9. Robert Archibald, a colleague from the Economics Department here at the College, served in Alpha Company two years after Charley Company eventuated the massacre at My Lai. His Company covered much the same territory as the old Charley Company, and he informs me that the kind of operation that went awry under Calley's leadership was routine. Moreover, many of the soldiers were angry with the villagers during these operations, but restraint was the norm, certainly nothing approaching the kind of response suggested as inevitable by Nussbaum's example.

10. Nussbaum, *The Therapy of Desire,* 403.

11. Ibid., 403.

12. It seems to me that the Stoic examples are not as good as Nussbaum's. If it is Nero and figures like him who are supposed to fix our intuitions regarding the excesses of public anger, one need only ask what the statistical probabilities are of duplicating that kind of psychology to arrive at the conclusion that the Stoic argumentative strategy is built on exaggeration. Perhaps this is understandable given the exaggerated times in which they lived. But building a philosophical position based on such exceptions is nothing short of foolish.

13. See Lucius Annaeus Seneca, *Medea,* trans. Moses Hadas (Indianapolis: Bobbs-Merrill, 1956).

CHAPTER 9

1. Oddly, it seems that Kantians sometimes encourage this line of thought, especially those who think that Kant's view requires us to compensate those who have been unfairly victimized by the natural lottery.

2. See Robert Nozick, *Anarchy, State, and Utopia* (New York: Basic Books, 1971), 142–145.

3. For a sampling, see Ronald J. Knapp, *Beyond Endurance: When a Child Dies* (New York: Schocken Books, 1986); Colin Murray Parkes, ed., *Bereavement: Studies of Grief in Adult Life* (New York: International Studies Press, 1972); and Wolfgang Stroebe and Margaret S. Stroebe, eds., *Bereavement and Health: The Psychological and Physical Consequences of Partner Loss* (Cambridge: Cambridge University Press, 1987).

4. See Miriam Griffin, *Seneca: A Philosopher in Politics* (Oxford: Clarendon Press, 1976).

Selected Bibliography

Allison, Henry E. *Kant's Theory of Freedom*. Cambridge: Cambridge University Press, 1990.

Annas, Julia. *Hellenistic Philosophy of Mind*. Berkeley: University of California Press, 1992.

———. *The Morality of Happiness*. New York: Oxford University Press, 1993.

Aristotle. *The Basic Works of Aristotle*. Edited by Richard McKeon. New York: Random House, 1941.

———. *Nicomachean Ethics*. Translated by Martin Ostwald. Indianapolis: Bobbs-Merrill, 1962.

———. *The Politics*. Edited by Stephen Everson. Cambridge: Cambridge University Press, 1988.

———. *On Rhetoric*. Translated by George A. Kennedy. New York: Oxford University Press, 1991.

Badhwar, Neera Kapur, ed. *Friendship: A Philosophical Reader*. Ithaca: Cornell University Press, 1993.

Baron, Marcia. *Kantian Ethics Almost Without Apology*. Ithaca: Cornell University Press, 1995.

Blum, Lawrence. *Friendship, Altruism, and Morality*. London: Routledge & Kegan Paul, 1980.

Brunschwig, Jacques. *Papers in Hellenistic Philosophy*. Translated by Janet Lloyd. New York: Cambridge University Press, 1994.

Cicero. *Selected Works*. Translated by Michael Grant. London: Penguin Books, 1960.

Cummiskey, David. *Kantian Consequentialism*. Oxford: Oxford University Press, 1996.

Donagan, Alan. *The Theory of Morality*. Chicago: University of Chicago Press, 1977.

Epicurus. *The Extant Remains.* Translated by Cyril Bailey. Oxford: Clarendon Press, 1926.

Frankfurt, Harry. *The Importance of What We Care About.* New York: Cambridge University Press, 1988.

Griffin, Miriam. *Seneca: A Philosopher in Politics.* Oxford: Clarendon Press, 1976.

Hadas, Moses, ed. *The Essential Works of Stoicism.* New York: Bantam Books, 1961.

Hardie, W. F. R. *Aristotle's Ethical Theory.* 2d ed. Oxford: Oxford University Press, 1980.

Harris, George. "Agent-centered Morality: Integrity and Human Agency." Manuscript.

——— . "Impartiality, Regulative Norms, and Practical Reason." Manuscript.

Herman, Barbara. *The Practice of Moral Judgment.* Cambridge: Harvard University Press, 1993.

Hill, Thomas. *Dignity and Practical Reason in Kant's Moral Theory.* Ithaca: Cornell University Press, 1992.

Kant, Immanuel. *Critique of Practical Reason.* Translated by Lewis White Beck. Indianapolis: Bobbs-Merrill, 1956.

——— . *The Doctrine of Virtue: Part II of the Metaphysics of Morals.* Translated by Mary J. Gregor. Philadelphia: University of Pennsylvania Press, 1964.

——— . *Groundwork of the Metaphysics of Morals.* Translated by H. J. Paton. New York: Harper Torchbooks, 1964.

——— . *Lectures on Ethics.* Translated by Louis Infield. Indianapolis: Hackett, 1930.

——— . *The Metaphysical Elements of Justice: Part I of The Metaphysics of Morals.* Translated by John Ladd. Indianapolis: Library of Liberal Arts, 1965.

——— . *Religion Within the Limits of Reason Alone.* Translated by Theodore M. Greene and Hoyt H. Hudson. New York: Harper Torchbooks, 1960.

Knapp, Ronald J. *Beyond Endurance: When a Child Dies.* New York: Schocken Books, 1986.

Long, A. A., and D. N. Sedley, eds. *The Hellenistic Philosophers.* Vol. 1: *Translations of the Principal Sources with Philosophical Commentary.* Cambridge: Cambridge University Press, 1987.

Lucretius. *On the Nature of the Universe.* Translated by R. E. Latham. London: Penguin Books, 1951.

Mistis, Phillip. *Epicurus' Ethical Theory: The Pleasures of Invulnerability.* Ithaca: Cornell University Press, 1988.

Nietzsche, Friedrich. *Beyond Good and Evil.* Translated by R. J. Hollingdale. London: Penguin Classics, 1973.

——— . *The Birth of Tragedy and the Genealogy of Morals.* Translated by Francis Golffing. New York: Doubleday Anchor Books, 1956.

——— . *The Genealogy of Morality.* Edited by Keith Ansell Pearson. Translated by Carol Diethe. New York: Cambridge University Press, 1994.

——— . *Twilight of the Idols and the Anti-Christ.* Translated by R. J. Hollingdale. London: Penguin Classics, 1968.

Nozick, Robert. *Anarchy, State, and Utopia.* New York: Basic Books, 1971.

Nussbaum, Martha. *The Fragility of Goodness: Luck and Ethics in Greek Tragedy and Philosophy.* Cambridge: Cambridge University Press, 1986.

———. *Love's Knowledge: Essays on Philosophy and Literature.* New York: Oxford University Press, 1990.

———. *The Therapy of Desire.* Princeton, N.J.: Princeton University Press, 1994.

O'Neill, Onora. *Constructions of Reason: Explorations of Kant's Practical Philosophy.* Cambridge: Cambridge University Press, 1989.

Pakaluk, Michael, ed. *Other Selves: Philosophers on Friendship.* Indianapolis: Hackett, 1989.

Parkes, Colin Murray, ed. *Bereavement: Studies of Grief in Adult Life.* New York: International Studies Press, 1972.

Posner, Gerald. *Hitler's Children.* New York: Random House, 1991.

Railton, Peter. "Alienation, Consequentialism, and the Demands of Morality." In *Friendship: A Philosophical Reader,* ed. Neera Kapur Badhwar, 211–244. Ithaca: Cornell University Press, 1993.

Rescher, Nicholas. "Noumenal Causality." In *Proceedings of the Third International Kant Congress,* ed. Lewis White Beck, 462–470. New York: Humanities Press, 1972.

Rist, John. *Stoic Philosophy.* Cambridge: Cambridge University Press, 1969.

Rorty, Amelie Oksenberg, ed. *Essays on Aristotle's Ethics.* Berkeley: University of California Press, 1980.

Seneca, Lucius Annaeus. *Letters from a Stoic.* Translated by Robin Campbell. London: Penguin Books, 1969.

———. *Medea.* Translated by Moses Hadas. Indianapolis: Bobbs-Merrill, 1956.

Sichrovsky, Peter. *Born Guilty.* Translated by Jean Steinberg. New York: Basic Books, 1988.

Solomon, Robert. *The Passions.* New York: Doubleday, 1976.

Stroebe, Wolfgang, and Margaret S. Stroebe, eds. *Bereavement and Health: The Psychological and Physical Consequences of Partner Loss.* Cambridge: Cambridge University Press, 1987.

Styron, William. *Sophie's Choice.* New York: Random House, 1976.

Unger, Peter. *Identity, Consciousness, and Value.* New York: Oxford University Press, 1990.

Williams, Bernard. *Ethics and the Limits of Philosophy.* Cambridge, Mass.: Harvard University Press, 1985.

———. *Moral Luck: Philosophical Papers 1973–1980.* Cambridge: Cambridge University Press, 1981.

———. *Problems of the Self.* Cambridge: Cambridge University Press, 1973.

———. "The Self and the Future." *Philosophical Review* 79 (1970): 161–180.

———. *Shame and Necessity.* Berkeley: University of California Press, 1993.

Wood, Allen W. "The Emptiness of the Moral Will." *Monist* 73 (1989): 454–483.

———. "Kant's Compatibilism." In *Self and Nature in Kant's Philosophy,* ed. Allen W. Wood, 73–101. Ithaca: Cornell University Press, 1984.

———. *Kant's Moral Religion.* Ithaca: Cornell University Press, 1970.

Index